obias

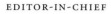

Mastering Your Fears and Phobias

SECOND EDITION

Therapist Guide

Michelle G. Craske • Martin M. Antony • David H. Barlow

OXFORD

UNIVERSITY PRESS

2006

OXFORD
UNIVERSITY PRESS

Oxford University Press, Inc., publishes works that further
Oxford University's objective of excellence
in research, scholarship, and education.

Oxford   New York
Auckland   Cape Town   Dar es Salaam   Hong Kong   Karachi
Kuala Lumpur   Madrid   Melbourne   Mexico City   Nairobi
New Delhi   Shanghai   Taipei   Toronto

With offices in
Argentina   Austria   Brazil   Chile   Czech Republic   France   Greece
Guatemala   Hungary   Italy   Japan   Poland   Portugal   Singapore
South Korea   Switzerland   Thailand   Turkey   Ukraine   Vietnam

Copyright © 2006 by Oxford University Press, Inc.

Published by Oxford University Press, Inc.
198 Madison Avenue, New York, New York 10016

www.oup.com

Library of Congress Cataloging-in-Publication Data
Craske, Michelle Genevieve, 1959–
Mastering your fears and phobias : therapist guide / Michelle G. Craske,
Martin M. Antony, David H. Barlow. —2nd ed.
p.   cm.—(Treatments that work)
Includes bibliographical references.
ISBN-13 978-0-19-518917-9
ISBN 0-19-518917-5
1. Phobias—Treatment.   2. Fear.   I. Antony, Martin M.
II. Barlow, David H.   III. Title.   IV. Series.
RC535.C74 2006
616.85'22506—dc22   2006007097

9 8 7 6 5 4 3 2 1

Printed in the United States of America
on acid-free paper

About Treatments *ThatWork*™

Stunning developments in healthcare have occurred in the last several years, but many of our widely accepted interventions and strategies in mental health and behavioral medicine have been brought into question by research evidence as not only lacking benefit but perhaps inducing harm. Other strategies have been proven effective using the best current standards of evidence, resulting in broad-based recommendations to make these practices more available to the public. Several recent developments are behind this revolution. First, we have arrived at a much deeper understanding of pathology, both psychological and physical, which has led to the development of new, more precisely targeted interventions. Second, our research methodologies have improved substantially, such that we have reduced threats to internal and external validity, making the outcomes more directly applicable to clinical situations. Third, governments around the world, healthcare systems, and policymakers have decided that the quality of care should improve, that it should be evidence-based, and that it is in the public's interest to ensure that this happens (Barlow, 2004; Institute of Medicine, 2001).

Of course, the major stumbling block for clinicians everywhere is the accessibility of newly developed evidence-based psychological interventions. Workshops and books can go only so far in acquainting responsible and conscientious practitioners with the latest behavioral healthcare practices and their applicability to individual patients. This new series, Treatments *ThatWork*™, is devoted to communicating these exciting new interventions to clinicians on the front lines of practice.

The manuals and workbooks in this series contain step-by-step detailed procedures for assessing and treating specific problems and diagnoses. But this series goes beyond the books and manuals by providing ancillary materials that will approximate the supervisory process to assist practitioners in the implementation of these procedures in their practice.

In our emerging healthcare system, the growing consensus is that evidence-based practice offers the most responsible course of action for the health professional. All behavioral healthcare clinicians deeply desire to provide the best possible care for their patients. In this series, our aim is to close the dissemination and information gap and make that possible.

This therapist guide and the companion workbook for clients address the treatment of specific phobias and fears. Specific phobias, which refer to fears that are of specific objects or situations and are severe enough to substantially interfere with an individual's functioning, comprise the most common anxiety disorder, estimated to affect 12.5% of the population. This problem is most often found in women, with almost 16% of women suffering substantial impairment from phobias. If one includes common fears that are distressing and somewhat disabling but do not meet the rigorous criteria for specific phobia, then these rates at least double; many of the individuals suffering from such fears could benefit from treatment as well. In many specific cases, such as blood, injury, and/or injection phobias, individuals are unable to receive appropriate medical or dental care and suffer the consequences. In other common phobias, such as those focused on transportation (driving, flying, etc.), clients miss out on a lifetime of opportunities to share significant events with family, follow desired career paths, and so on.

There is wide consensus on the efficacy and effectiveness of one, and only one, treatment for specific phobia: this is the cognitive behavioral exposure–based strategy that addresses both external and internal fear cues as outlined in this workbook. With this approach, one can be successful up to 90% of the time with as little as one day to one week of treatment. Since most phobias are chronic and lifelong, this is a remarkably efficient and effective treatment—one of the most effective found in all of healthcare. And yet very few therapists offer this service to their clients. We sincerely hope that this up-to-date therapist guide and accompanying workbook assists clinicians everywhere to make their clients aware of this service and to offer it more frequently.

David H. Barlow, Editor-in-Chief,
Treatments *ThatWork*™
Boston, Massachusetts

Acknowledgments

The authors thank Julia Blood for her help preparing the original manuscript for revision and suggesting sections to be updated. Thanks also to Mariclaire Cloutier, Cristina Wojdylo, and the staff at Oxford University Press for their support and expertise.

Contents

Mastering Your Fears and Phobias

Chapter 1   *Introductory Information for Therapists*

Background Information and Purpose of This Program

The program outlined in this manual is geared toward people who suffer from fears of circumscribed objects or situations, including animals, insects, closed-in places, driving, flying, heights, blood, injury or injection, and other common objects or situations. It is ideal for those who suffer from specific phobia, as defined in *Diagnostic and Statistical Manual of Mental Disorders–Fourth Edition* (*DSM–IV*) (American Psychiatric Association, 2000). However, it is likely also useful for fears that are intense but do not interfere with daily functioning, or even for fears that are not so severe.

This therapist guide includes a description of the major points from each chapter in the accompanying *Mastering Your Fears and Phobias* (MYFP) *Workbook,* as well as the primary information to be conveyed by the therapist and the principles underlying the therapeutic procedures described in each chapter. Also included in this guide are typical questions asked by clients, and issues that may arise in each chapter.

Although the workbook is written for the client, a mental health professional should supervise the treatment because many of the concepts and procedures are relatively complex. The most effective implementation requires a familiarity with the nature of specific phobias and the basic principles of cognitive and behavioral intervention to adapt the various lessons to each client's needs. Therefore, the mental health professional should be fully familiar with the workbook and aware of the conceptual bases for the different therapeutic techniques. Consult the references and recommended readings listed at the end of this therapist guide for more in-depth information about cognitive behavioral treatment principles.

Prevalence

Mild fears of specific situations and objects are quite common in the general population (Curtis, Magee, Eaton, Wittchen, & Kessler, 1998); however, specific phobias (that cause clinically significant interference and/or distress) are among the most common anxiety disorders. The National Comorbidity Survey lifetime prevalence rate for specific phobias, using *DSM–IV* criteria, was 12.5% (Kessler, Berglund, Demler, Jin, & Walters, 2005).

Gender

Women (15.7%) are more likely than men (6.7%) to be diagnosed with a specific phobia (Kessler et al., 1994). Overall, 75–90% of individuals with animal, natural environment, or situational-specific phobia are women, as are 55–70% of individuals with phobias of heights, blood, or injections (Himle, McPhee, Cameron, & Curtis, 1989).

Age of Onset, Course, and Demographic Characteristics

Most individuals with animal-, blood-, or –injection-specific phobia report an onset of difficulties in childhood, whereas situational and natural-environment phobias tend to begin later, often in adolescence or early adulthood (for a review, see Antony & Barlow, 2002). Additionally, for those phobias beginning during childhood, the phobias tend to intensify between the ages of 10 and 13 (Strauss & Last, 1993). Untreated specific phobias tend to be chronic, with a remission rate over a seven-year period as low as 16% (Wittchen, 1988).

Below, we summarize the key features of specific phobia, based on criteria from the *DSM–IV.* Note that this condition was called "simple phobia" in earlier editions.

1. The individual has an extreme and persistent fear that is excessive or unrealistic and that is triggered by a particular object or situation, such as flying, being at a height, encountering animals, receiving an injection, or seeing blood.

2. The individual experiences an immediate anxiety response (which may take the form of a panic attack) almost every time he or she encounters the phobic object or situation. In children, the anxiety may be expressed by symptoms such as tantrums, crying, clinging, or freezing.

3. The individual recognizes that his or her fear is excessive or unreasonable, though in children this feature may be absent.

4. The individual avoids the feared object or situation, or endures it with intense anxiety or distress.

5. The anxiety, avoidance, or distress related to the feared object or situation leads to significant impairment in the individual's functioning, or the individual is significantly distressed about having the phobia.

6. In individuals under age 18, the problem must last at least six months.

Also, the anxiety, panic attacks, or phobic avoidance associated with the specific object or situation must not be better accounted for by another mental disorder, such as *obsessive-compulsive disorder* (e.g., a person may fear animals as part of a larger fear of contamination), *posttraumatic stress disorder* (e.g., a person may fear driving because he or she does not want to be reminded of a previous car accident), *separation anxiety disorder* (e.g., a person avoids school for fear of being separated from parents), *social phobia* (e.g., a person fears driving, but the fear is exclusively secondary to a fear of being embarrassed, humiliated, or criticized by others on the road), *panic disorder with agoraphobia,* or *agoraphobia without history of panic disorder* (e.g., the person fears flying because he or she fears having an unexpected panic attack on an airplane and not being able to escape).

Historically, the various specific phobias (e.g., animals, heights, blood, flying) were grouped together, but research suggesting marked differences across the various types of phobias (Himle et al., 1989; Öst, 1987) has led to four main types of specific phobias in *DSM–IV:* animal fears (e.g., dogs, cats, snakes, spiders, birds, insects), natural-environment fears (e.g., storms, heights, water), blood- or injection-injury fears (e.g., receiving or observing injections, blood, surgery, injury), and situational fears (e.g., flying, driving, enclosed spaces). These types tend to differ in terms of age of onset (Antony, Brown, & Barlow, 1997a; Öst, 1987), rates of comorbidity with other disorders (Himle et al., 1989), response profiles (Antony, Brown, & Barlow, 1997a, 1997b), familial aggregation (Himle et al., 1989), and genetic variance (Kendler, Neale, Kessler, Heath, & Eaves, 1992). A fifth "other" type is included in *DSM–IV* to describe phobias that do not easily fit into one of these types (e.g., choking and vomiting phobias).

When individuals with specific phobias are *not* exposed to their feared object or situation, they experience the *least* severe and impairing anxiety disorder (Antony & Barlow, 2002). However, when encountering their feared objects or situations, individuals with phobias tend to experience severe discomfort and may attempt to escape from the situation or endure it with great distress. This distress is often accompanied by physical symptoms such as palpitations, sweating, blushing, and trembling, which may take the form of a situationally bound panic attack. Individuals may also experience similar distress in advance or in anticipation of exposure to a feared situation or object (e.g., before a scheduled flight, prior to a medical appointment). As a result, feared situations are often avoided. Such fear and avoidance may significantly interfere with the individual's functioning, often resulting in a change in normal routines, decline in occupational opportunities, negative impact on social relationships, or changes in regular health maintenance behaviors (e.g., medical checkups).

Fear and Anxiety

At this point, it is useful to distinguish fear from anxiety (Barlow, 1988, 2000; American Psychiatric Association, 2000). Fear is the emotion the individual experiences when directly confronted with threat or danger and is associated with strong, protective behavioral action tendencies (flight or fight). Panic is the occurrence of fear when there is no objective threat. Thus, most phobic reactions would be severe enough to meet criteria for a situationally bound (or cued) panic attack. Anxiety, on the other hand, is a future-oriented state characterized by worry, tension, and hypervigilance about future threat. Thus, individuals with specific phobia experience substantial anxiety, usually called "anticipatory anxiety," if faced with the prospect of confronting their phobic object or situation again.

Development of This Treatment Program and Evidence Base

The development of behavioral treatments for circumscribed phobias have their roots largely in the work of Joseph Wolpe, M.D., whose book *Psychotherapy by Reciprocal Inhibition* described the therapeutic methods and successes of *systematic desensitization* (Wolpe, 1958). Systematic desensitization entails repeatedly pairing phobic stimuli that are progressively more anxiety provoking with a competing response of relaxation. Wolpe believed that, through a process called *reciprocal inhibition* (or, *counterconditioning*), the relaxation response inhibited the anxiety response, so that the phobic stimulus could be imagined without anxiety. Such imaginal counterconditioning was presumed to then generalize to real-life encounters with the phobic stimulus.

The efficacy of systematic desensitization, in comparison to insight-oriented psychotherapies and no-treatment controls, was demonstrated across a large number of independently conducted investigations throughout the 1960s and 1970s. Systematic desensitization in its original form continues to be used by some clinicians, though most behaviorally oriented therapists tend to use more-modern exposure-based treatments that evolved from systematic desensitization. Research investigating the purported therapeutic mechanisms of systematic desensitization demonstrated that (a) similar rates of success were achieved from repeated imaginings of phobic stimuli without the involvement of relaxation training, and (b) similar and sometimes superior efficacy was obtained from repeated exposures to real-life (in contrast to imagined) phobic stimuli (e.g., Barlow, Leitenberg, Agras, & Wincze, 1969).

These findings led to a burgeoning of "exposure-based" procedures, involving repeated confrontation with actual phobic stimuli. Overall, exposure-based treatments are highly effective for a wide range of specific phobias, including fears of spiders (Antony, McCabe, Leeuw, Sano, & Swinson, 2001; Hellström & Öst, 1995; Muris, Mayer, & Merckelbach, 1998; Mystkowski, Craske, & Echiverri, 2002; Mystkowski, Echiverri, Labus, & Craske, in press; Öst, Ferebee, & Furmark, 1997; Öst, Salkovskis, & Hellström, 1991; Rowe & Craske, 1998; Tsao & Craske, 2001), snakes (Craske, Mohlman, Yi, Glover, & Valeri, 1995; Gauthier & Marshall, 1977; Hepner & Cauthen, 1975), rats (Foa, Blau, Prout, & Latimer, 1977), thunder and lightning (Öst, 1978), water (Menzies & Clarke, 1993), heights (Baker, Cohen, & Saunders, 1973; Bourque & Ladouceur, 1980; Lang & Craske, 2000), flying (Beckham, Vrana, May, Gustafson, & Smith, 1990; Howard, Murphy, & Clarke, 1983; Öst, Brandberg, & Alm, 1997), enclosed places (Öst, Johansson, & Jerremalm, 1982; Craske et al., 1995), choking (Greenberg, Stern, & Weilburg, 1988), dental treatment (Gitin, Herbert, & Schmidt, 1996; Moore & Brødsgaard, 1994), blood (Öst, Fellenius, & Sterner, 1991), and balloons (Houlihan, Schwartz, Miltenberger, & Heuton, 1993).

In fact, concentrated, single-session exposure treatments are highly effective for arachnophobia (Hellström & Öst, 1995; Öst, Ferebee, & Furmark, 1997; Öst, Salkovskis, & Hellström, 1991), blood phobia (Hellström, Fellenius, & Öst, 1996), injection phobia (Öst, Hellström, & Kaver, 1992), and flying phobia (Öst, Brandberg, & Alm, 1997). These brief treatments are effective even in group formats, although smaller groups tend to yield better outcomes than larger groups (Öst, 1996). While results from one-session treatments maintain over long intervals, maintenance may depend on continued exposure. For example, Liddell, di Fazio, Blackwood, and Ackerman (1994) followed dental phobics in 1990 who had been successfully treated from 1985 to 1989: those who did not continue to see a dentist regularly did less well.

Clearly, behavioral treatments are the treatments of choice for specific phobias. Meta-analyses indicate very strong effect sizes with results being stable for at least one year after treatment (Ruhmland & Margraf, 2001). Of course, there is still room for improvement, such as the development of strategies to ensure the maintenance of therapeutic gains over longer and longer periods of time, and the possible combination of behavioral and pharmacological approaches for those individuals who prefer an anxiolytic-medication aid for overcoming phobias.

Several recent advances have further enhanced the efficacy of exposure treatments for specific phobias. First, significant advances have occurred with respect to information-processing biases, or biases in judgment and attention. Specifically, it is now well understood that specific phobias are associated with an attentional bias to preferentially allocate attentional resources to phobic stimuli and with tendencies to inflate the perceived danger associated with phobic stimuli. Recent evidence indicates that exposure-based procedures for specific phobias are sometimes enhanced when combined with cognitive restructuring designed to correct the tendencies to inflate the perceived danger associated with phobic stimuli. In fact, cognitive restructuring is sometimes sufficient for anxiety reduction, at least with respect to one type of phobia, claustrophobia (Booth & Rachman, 1992) and there is some evidence that cognitive procedures enhance exposure-based approaches (Emmelkamp & Felten, 1985). The treatment in this program incorporates basic elements of cognitive restructuring to facilitate exposure therapy.

Second, exposure as a method has been facilitated by virtual-reality technology, which has been shown in a few studies to be as effective as real-life exposure treatments (particularly for phobias of flying and heights), although it is unclear whether that effectiveness is attributable to self-directed in-vivo exposure, or whether virtual reality is sufficient in the absence of in-vivo exposure. There is information about virtual reality treatments in several sections of the workbook.

Third, there have been advances with respect to the biobehavioral mechanisms of fear extinction, which has relevance to the process of exposure therapy for treating specific phobias. For example, an interesting recent development in conditioning theory was first proposed by Bouton (1993) and has now been well supported in basic research with rodents and in clinical research with humans (see Hermans, Craske, Mineka, & Lovibond, in press). The original excitatory (i.e., dangerous) meaning of the conditional stimulus is not erased during extinction, but rather an additional inhibitory (i.e., nondangerous) meaning is learned. Thus, extinction results in previously feared stimulus having two meanings (danger and nondanger). Fear will be expressed in the future if the original, danger, meaning is evoked. Meanings are evoked by the surrounding context. Thus, a snake may represent danger in the back yard but nondanger in the therapist's office. The importance of context dependency lies in the proposition that fear is likely to return if the client encounters the phobic stimulus post-treatment in a context that is distinctly different from the treatment context. Although the evidence is preliminary, there are some data to suggest that such context-specific effects can be offset by conducting exposure therapy in all the contexts in which the phobic stimulus is likely to be encountered in the future (see Vansteenwegen, Dirikx, Hermans, Vervliet, & Eelen, in press). However, should fear return, reinstituting all treatment principles described herein is the most important step, as is described when discussing maintenance of treatment gains in the workbook.

Another key development in the biobehavioral mechanisms of fear extinction and exposure therapy is recognition that the degree to which reported fear or anxiety decreases during a trial of exposure therapy is not a sign of learning and therefore is not predictive of how much fear is experienced the next time the phobic stimulus is encountered (see Craske & Mystkowski, 2006). This is an important development because it means a basic shift in the way in which exposure therapy is conducted. Instead of focusing on remaining in the phobic situation until fear declines, we now recognize the value of designing exposures in such a way that they promote corrective learning regardless of how much fear is experienced, even if that means fear is sustained throughout exposure. Therefore, the instruction is no longer to stay in the situation until fear declines but rather to stay in the situation for the length of time or the number of times necessary to learn that what clients are most worried about never or rarely happens, or for clients to learn that they can cope with the phobic stimulus and with their anxiety. Fear and anxiety will eventually diminish as a result of structuring exposures in this way. These instructions are incorporated throughout the workbook.

A final development in the biobehavioral mechanisms of fear extinction is the recent use of D-cycloserine, a cognitive enhancer, which appears to facilitate exposure and the extinction of conditioned fear (Ressler et al., 2004; Walker, Ressler, Lu, & Davis, 2002). However, given the early stage of research on this cognitive enhancer, this treatment program does not discuss the use of D-cycloserine.

As already stated, heterogeneity among the different types of phobias is now recognized in the *DSM–IV*: blood, injury, and injection phobias; situational phobias (driving, flying, closed-in situations); natural-environment phobias (heights, dark, water, storms); and animal and insect phobias (spiders, snakes, cats). This leads to differences in the way that treatment is tailored to each type of phobia. For example, blood, injury, and injection phobias are characterized by a "diphasic" autonomic response pattern in which an initial increase in arousal is followed by a decrease in heart rate and blood pressure that is often associated with fainting in these individuals. Consequently, Lars-Göran Öst and his colleagues (Öst, Fellenius, & Stemer, 1991) have shown that applied tension is a very effective technique for treating blood, injury, and injection phobias by helping individuals raise their blood pressure and thereby avoid fainting. Öst, Sterner, & Fellenius (1989) concluded that applied tension should be the treatment of choice for blood phobia. Öst et al. (1991) dismantled applied tension by comparing applied tension as previously conducted (exposure with tensing), to exposure without tensing, and to tension without exposure. Each condition lasted five sessions. Overall, tension alone was almost as effective as applied tension, while exposure alone was considerably less effective. Thus, tension as a coping skill may be more important than exposure in the case of blood and injection phobias associated with fainting.

As another example, fears of closed-in situations share many features with panic disorder and agoraphobia, such as panic attacks and anxiety over the physical feelings of suffocation and shortness of breath. As a result, elements of the treatments for panic disorder that focus on overcoming fears of bodily sensations (see *Mastery of Your Anxiety and Panic, Fourth Edition*, Barlow & Craske, 2006) have been incorporated in the treatment for claustrophobia with some success. In fact, the incorporation of panic-control strategies is helpful for any specific phobia in which the individual is fearful not only of the external phobic object or situation but also of his or her own physical sensations.

Comorbidity: What If Other Problems Are Present?

It is not at all uncommon for people with specific phobias to have other anxiety disorders, such as social phobia, panic disorder, or generalized anxiety disorder. The additional problems do not preclude treatment with this program. Generally, we recommend dealing with the most distressing and disabling anxiety disorder first. For example, if a client presents with a specific phobia and social phobia, it is appropriate to proceed with the MYFP program for the specific phobia if the specific phobia is causing more distress or impairment of functioning than the social phobia. On the other hand, if the social phobia is clearly more severe and disabling than the specific phobia, then the social phobia should be treated first.

The treatment in the workbook targets phobic anticipation, fear, and avoidance behavior. It does not address other issues that may in some cases be relevant, such as major life stresses or physical complications. Nor does the treatment address accompanying mood states such as depression. It is for this reason that we recommend that, when implementing the program, the focus be limited to dealing with fear and avoidance of circumscribed stimuli. If other emotional problems are primary, or if life crises emerge, we recommend that they be dealt with before attempting to control specific phobic reactions.

Differential Diagnosis: Is It a Specific Phobia?

Phobic reactions are common to almost all anxiety disorders. Therefore, it is sometimes difficult to separate a true specific phobia from a phobic reaction that is part of another anxiety disorder.

For example, someone who obsesses over cleanliness may be phobic of public telephones or door handles in public buildings because they fear dirt and germs. The individual may also avoid touching certain animals, for fear of contamination. However, rather than reflecting a specific phobia, fears of contamination, dirt, or germs are more likely to reflect obsessive-compulsive disorder. Similarly, excessive fears of injuring other people are usually classified as part of an obsessive-compulsive disorder. For these kinds of symptom presentations, we recommend the Treatments *That Work*™ program *Mastery of Obsessive-Compulsive Disorder.*

Persons with panic disorder and agoraphobia are typically phobic of many of the same situations as people with specific situational phobias (e.g., flying, driving, being in crowded places). The person who fears or avoids these situations in addition to other situations, such as being alone or being away from medical help, is more likely to be suffering from agoraphobia, particularly if the fear and avoidance is due to fear of panic attacks or related bodily sensations and if the person worries pervasively about panic attacks. Furthermore, panic disorder with agoraphobia is typically associated with panic attacks that are not triggered by any specific situation or object but that seem to occur "out of the blue." We recommend our Treatments *That Work*™ program *Mastery of Your Anxiety and Panic, Third Edition* (Barlow & Craske, 2000) for individuals who are suffering from panic disorder with agoraphobia. Some people with specific phobias panic when they are confronted with their phobic stimulus, and thus the experience of a panic attack is not an immediate diagnostic rule-out for the specific phobia diagnosis. However, specific phobias are not connected with worry about panic attacks outside the phobic situation.

Social phobia refers to fear and avoidance of situations because of concern about being embarrassed, humiliated, or judged negatively by others. Social anxiety may cause a person to fear and avoid crowds, parties, interviews, telephone calls, or public speaking. We have also seen socially anxious individuals who fear driving (e.g., they fear other drivers' judging their driving skills); in this case, they typically fear numerous other social situations. Usually, if one avoids a situation for fear of being embarrassed, humiliated, or judged by others, social phobia is a more appropriate diagnosis than is specific phobia. For example, a person who avoids flying for fear of having to talk to the person next to him or her and also avoids other social situations might have social phobia. However, a person who avoids flying for fear of crashing is more likely to have a specific phobia of flying. We recommend the Treatments *That Work*™ program *Managing Social Anxiety,* for individuals who are suffering from social phobia.

Posttraumatic stress disorder (a reaction to a severe stressor such as being attacked or seeing someone else get badly hurt) can result in phobic reactions also. For example, the woman whose rapist smelled of cigar smoke may develop a phobia of cigar smoke, and the combat veteran may develop phobias of the sounds of gunshots or planes flying overhead. However, in posttraumatic stress disorder, the phobic reactions are accompanied by other symptoms, such as re-experiencing the trauma (e.g., flashbacks and nightmares). We recommend the Treatments *That Work*™ programs that relate to trauma recovery (e.g., *Overcoming the Trauma of Your Motor Vehicle Accident* or *Reclaiming Your Life After Rape*) for individuals who are suffering from posttraumatic stress disorder.

Finally, a *delusion* may result in phobic behavior. Delusions are false beliefs that are firmly held and are based on an incorrect interpretation of reality that persists despite obvious proof that the belief is false. For example, the delusion that other drivers on the road are intent on crashing into one's own car may lead to extreme fear and avoidance of driving. However, in contrast to delusions, specific phobic reactions are typically recognized by the person as being excessive or out of proportion to reality (although this recognition may not be apparent in children who are phobic).

Mental health professionals may wish to screen clients using the *Anxiety Disorders Interview Schedule for DSM–IV* (ADIS–IV) (Brown, Di Nardo, & Barlow, 1994), which is useful for teasing apart differential anxiety disorder diagnoses. Specifically, this semistructured interview identifies the nature of the anxiety or panic, determines whether one or more anxiety and mood disorders is present, and ascertains the relative severity of these disorders. (This interview is available from Oxford University Press and is part of the Treatments *That Work*™ series).

The Role of Medications

Medications are generally considered to be of limited benefit for specific phobias (Roy-Byrne & Cowley, in press). The few studies that have been conducted have mostly found no benefit from incorporating pharmacological treatments with behavioral treatments, and one study has shown that the use of benzodiazepines may reduce the therapeutic effects of exposure treatment (Wilhelm & Roth, 1997). Though one study

(Benjamin, Ben-Zion, Karbofsky, & Dannon, 2000) found that paroxetine ($n = 5$) was more effective than a placebo ($n = 6$) in individuals with specific phobias, the main outcome measures were scales that are typically used to assess other forms of anxiety (e.g., agoraphobia, social phobia, generalized anxiety), and the number of people in each condition was too small for statistical analyses to be meaningful. Furthermore, given that the evidence for the efficacy of behavioral treatments for specific phobias is overwhelming even in the absence of pharmacological treatments, it is widely believed that medication is not necessary to treat clients with specific phobias.

If a client is taking a stable dosage of medication to treat their phobia, we typically recommend that he or she continue to take the same dosage during the initial stages of behavioral treatment and, later, taper the medication under the supervision of the prescribing physician. During medication discontinuation, additional sessions of cognitive behavioral treatment may help clients manage unpleasant symptoms of withdrawal. For clients taking medication on an "as needed" or PRN basis, it is preferable to conduct exposure practices without the medication. There is some evidence that clients who attribute their successes to medication are less likely to maintain their gains than clients who attribute their success to exposure-based treatment (Başoğlu, Marks, Kiliç, Brewin, & Swinson, 1994).

Dealing With the Therapist's Own Fear

Occasionally, the therapist may find that he or she shares a client's discomfort with a particular object or situation. For example, a therapist who is treating an individual with a spider phobia might find that he or she is uncomfortable touching a spider. It is important for the therapist to be able to model nonfearful behavior when treating individuals with specific phobias. Therefore, it is recommended that therapists spend some time exposing themselves to the phobic object or situation until their own fears have subsided. If the therapist's own fear is particularly intense, it might be necessary to refer the client to another therapist who is better able to deal with the feared object or situation.

Group Versus Individual Sessions

Most research studies of treatments for specific phobias use individual treatment formats; in the experience of the authors, individual treatment is the treatment of choice. Nevertheless, treatment can be conducted in groups, in which case the following guidelines are useful:

1. Each group member should receive a behavioral test to assess his or her response to the phobic object or situation. Individuals whose reaction might be disruptive or frightening to other group members (e.g., excessive crying, screaming, or fainting) should undergo exposure therapy individually, rather than in a group.

2. Limit the group to no more than six clients, as larger groups make it difficult for the therapist to allocate sufficient attention to each client during a 90-minute session.

3. Use a co-therapist, if possible, so that clients can receive adequate individual attention.

Use of the Workbook

The workbook was designed for clients to use in tandem with their therapist's implementation of this therapist guide. The MYFP program is a scientifically sound treatment guide, written at the client's level, that can be a valuable supplement to a program delivered by professionals from a number of disciplines.

The MYFP program is divided into three parts. The first part of the workbook explains the nature of fear and specific phobias and describes how a phobia develops, factors that account for the persistence of phobias over time, and characteristics of different types of phobias. The second part of the workbook outlines general treatment procedures, giving a rationale and overview of the steps involved. The third part includes detailed descriptions of the treatment procedures for the various specific phobias. Clients should read the first two parts, and then focus on the chapters in the third part that deal with their own specific phobias.

The first two parts of the workbook comprise seven chapters. Because these parts are mostly informational rather than applied, the material from these chapters can be combined and discussed over two or three therapy sessions, or even assigned for reading between sessions. The therapist should describe the principles relevant to each chapter and ask clients to spend time before the next therapy session reading the relevant chapters and completing the practice exercises as specified. Usually, the therapist will meet with the client weekly and assign readings and exercises to complete before the next meeting. Although weekly sessions are typical, specific phobias can be treated more intensively, with several sessions per week. Either way, most of the sessions are typically spent on exposure to the feared object or situation. In fact, as reviewed earlier, clients with certain types of specific phobia (e.g., animal phobias, blood phobias) will often respond well to a single session of exposure lasting two to three hours. Cognitive strategies can be integrated into the treatment as needed.

In the thrid part, a separate chapter is devoted to each main specific phobia. The length of time it takes to complete a chapter in this part depends on the client's response to the treatment. For example, a fear of spiders may be overcome in just one week of daily, lengthy practice with spiders. On the other hand, fears of flying may take longer to overcome, largely because it is difficult to conduct repeated flying practices. Also, some clients prefer to practice with their phobic object or situation more gradually, in which cased treatment takes longer.

The advantages to using a manual-based program include:

1. *Self-paced progress.* Clients can move at their own pace. It was noted earlier that some therapists and clients prefer to shorten the program by scheduling more frequent sessions or by taking a more intense approach. Others, for a variety of reasons, choose to move more slowly. It can be quite helpful for a client to have the workbook for review between irregularly scheduled sessions.

2. *Clients can refer to the workbook when necessary.* A client who seems to understand material during the session may later become confused or forget information. One of the greatest benefits of the workbook is that it allows clients to review relevant concepts and instructions between treatment sessions to consolidate their learning.

3. *Family members and friends can read the workbook.* Research studies have demonstrated the benefits of involving family members, particularly spouses or other partners, in the treatment of several anxiety disorders, including agoraphobia and obsessive-compulsive disorder. For example, the authors have found that clients with panic disorder with agoraphobia whose partners were involved in treatment did better, based on results of a two-year follow-up, than did clients whose partners were not included. The client workbook describes how family or friends can serve as coaches to help clients overcome their fears and phobias. Including family and friends accomplishes several things. First, attempts to sabotage the program, either purposefully or unwittingly, seem to be minimized if family members are familiar with the nature of the problem and the rationale behind the various exercises included in the treatment. Second, as explicitly outlined in this manual, family or friends can help clients overcome some of their avoidance behavior by serving as role models, team problem solvers, and coaches. Of course, there are some clients who prefer that their partners or family or friends remain unaware of their problem. In these cases, we try to persuade clients of the advantages of sharing the problem with their partner and attempt to allay their concerns. Typically, these concerns involve worries that their family will think they are crazy or will be openly hostile to their efforts. This rarely happens, although there are cases in which a client's concerns about including a family member are realistic. When the therapist and client agree that involving the spouse may be beneficial, the spouse can be brought into the sessions, either initially, or throughout the whole treatment, and incorporated more fully as a coach. If it appears that the family member is unwilling or unable to be supportive during exposure practices (if, for example, there are marital problems, or the partner is also phobic), the therapist should help the client find another family member or friend who might help.

4. *Clients can refer to the workbook after the program ends.* The MYFP program prepares clients for the phobia's possible recurrence. Reviewing the material in the workbook can greatly comfort clients during these periods and can prevent the escalation of fear and avoidance.

Every client should complete every chapter in the first two parts of the workbook, even if some of the sections are less relevant than others. The material presented in these parts forms the basis for the active intervention in the last part. It is reiterated throughout the workbook that in-vivo exposure to the feared object or situation is essential for everyone. In addition, cognitive restructuring to correct misappraisals about the feared objects and situations is likely to be helpful for most people, whereas exposure to overcome fears of bodily sensations in the phobic context may be more relevant for some individuals than for others. Hence, it is important to conduct a careful functional analysis of each person's phobia to determine how much emphasis to place on each of the main treatment intervention strategies (i.e., exposure to the phobic stimulus, cognitive restructuring, and exposure to feared bodily sensations).

Introduction to Specific Phobias and Their Treatment

Chapter 2 | *Specific Phobias: Phenomenology*

(Corresponds to chapter 1 of the workbook)

Outline

■ Provide information about specific phobias

■ Help the client understand the different types of phobias

■ Describe the type of client who may benefit from this treatment

■ List the costs and benefits of treatment

Educating patients about the different types of phobias and their prevalence, comorbidity, and so on, begins the process of objective self-awareness. To observe and understand one's fear reactions from an objective standpoint facilitates a problem-solving approach to overcoming fear.

Information About Specific Phobias

Descriptive information about specific phobias is intended to reassure clients that phobic reactions are not very different from normal fear, except that they occur to a degree that is out of proportion with the actual dangers of the situation and that the fear leads to clinically significant impairment or distress.

Important points to emphasize to the client include:

■ Phobias are very common. It is estimated that 12.5% of the general population suffers from at least one specific phobia at some time in their lifetimes (Kessler et al., 2005).

■ People frequently have more than one phobia at a time.

A phobia differs from a nonclinical fear in several ways. First, a phobia represents excessive fear, or a level of fear that is above and beyond the actual dangerousness of a situation. Second, a phobia is fear that interferes with a person's life or preferred activities, or that is so distressing as to lessen the enjoyment of usual activities. The interference could affect daily activities or major life decisions (such as employment or residence).

Specific phobias differ from other anxiety disorders, even though other anxiety disorders can involve phobic-like reactions. A specific phobia is different from a general fear of contamination, self-doubt, or a fear of harming others (i.e., obsessive-compulsive disorder); a fear of being away from help or safety or of having a panic attack (i.e., agoraphobia); a fear of being evaluated negatively by others (i.e., social phobia); or a fear of being reminded of a severely traumatic past event (i.e., posttraumatic stress disorder).

A person who is phobic may either avoid the feared object or situation or endure the object or situation with considerable anticipatory anxiety and distress during confrontation.

The *DSM–IV* diagnostic criteria for specific phobia state that the fear is related to a very specific object or situation (i.e., it is circumscribed); the fear is persistent and excessive; exposure to the object or situation produces an almost immediate anxiety response that may or may not develop into a panic attack; the adult sufferer recognizes that the fear is irrational; and the feared object or situation is avoided or endured with intense anxiety that interferes with the person's functioning. Furthermore, the phobic reaction is diagnosed as a specific phobia only when it is not better accounted for by another mental disorder. (See point about other anxiety disorders and section on *Atypical and Problematic Responses,* below.)

Different Types of Phobias

There are several distinguishable types of specific phobias. These include animal phobias (e.g., fears of dogs, cats, mice, birds, snakes, bugs, spiders, and other animals); natural-environment phobias (e.g., fear of heights, dark, water, and storms); situational phobias (e.g., fear of traveling by car, train, bus, plane, or boats, or of closed-in or claustrophobic situations), blood, injection, and injury phobias, and a miscellaneous category for other phobias. These different types of phobias are distinguished in the *DSM–IV* (American Psychiatric Association, 2000) because of their different patterns of age of onset, comorbidity with other disorders, symptomatology, and possible treatment response.

Who Will Benefit From This Treatment?

The MYFP program is most appropriate for individuals who fear circumscribed objects or situations to a degree that is excessive or unrealistic, interferes with life or causes a lot of distress, and is not part of another anxiety disorder. As with all treatment approaches, the MYFP program, although empirically supported, may not be appropriate for all clients. The workbook informs the client of alternative treatments.

Costs and Benefits of This Program

The description of costs and benefits is intended to convey to clients that although the program may be very helpful for them, it will take some work. In other words, they are encouraged to have realistic expectations of how much work is involved and to be prepared and motivated for the effort needed. Clients are informed that learning to overcome excessive fear entails learning new skills and learning to change patterns of behavior, as opposed to only developing insights.

It is valuable to explain to clients that the costs of participation in the MYFP program include the time and effort involved and possible initial increases in anxiety as phobic objects are confronted. The benefits of involvement include overcoming a specific phobia, increased quality of life, and improved self-esteem. With such information, clients can make an informed choice about initiating treatment and increasing their investment in treatment.

Case Vignettes

Case Vignette 1

C: I must be crazy to be so afraid of lizards. I know they can't hurt me, but they terrify me.

T: By definition, phobias are fears that persist despite the recognition that they are irrational or illogical. This is quite different from being "crazy." It is probably the case that your choice to stay away from lizards convinces you on an emotional level to be afraid, even though your logical mind tells you that you don't need to be afraid.

Case Vignette 2

C: I am so afraid of heights that I can't look at television shows of people climbing rock faces, or shots of deep canyons, or anything like that. Is that usual?

T: Yes. When fear is intense, it can generalize to things that remind you of what you fear or represent it in some way. Imagining being up high, seeing someone else up high, or viewing panoramic views from a height represent the situation that you fear and, therefore, may produce some discomfort.

Case Vignette 3

C: I have been so afraid of flying for so long that it is hard for me to imagine ever being able to fly again.

T: Fortunately, the treatments for circumscribed fears and phobias are generally very effective, as long as you stick with the exercises that are assigned and work hard at learning ways of overcoming your fear. The length of time that you have had a phobia is less important for treatment success than how much effort you put into overcoming your phobia.

Case Vignette 4

C: I feel so embarrassed. Here I am a successful entrepreneur who flies around the world on business trips, and yet I am afraid to drive on the freeway.

T: The nature of specific phobias is fear of very circumscribed objects or situations, so it is very common to have a strong fear of just one or two situations, with very little discomfort in most other areas of daily functioning.

Case Vignette 5

C: Is there any kind of drug you can give me to help me over this problem—I just can't stand the feeling of being trapped inside an elevator.

T: Some people prefer to use medications to help them overcome their fears. This program helps you control your fears by learning new ways of thinking, feeling, and acting. Medications usually take less effort, but evidence suggests that cognitive behavioral treatments (like this one) are very effective for treating specific phobias and have longer-lasting effects than medications.

Case Vignette 6

C: Why isn't anyone else afraid?

T: Almost everyone has at least a mild fear of one thing or another. Although others may appear not to be afraid, they would most likely confess to something they fear if you questioned them enough. Remember, fears are very common.

Troubleshooting

The most problematic issue initially is deciding whether using *Mastering Your Fears and Phobias* is appropriate, because differential diagnostic issues sometimes pose problems. The overlap between a series of specific phobias and agoraphobia, for example, can be difficult to disentangle. Careful interviewing, perhaps with the aid of the ADIS–IV diagnostic interview (Brown, Di Nardo, & Barlow, 1994), and assurance that the specific fears are not part of another anxiety disorder (such as obsessive-compulsive disorder, agoraphobia, posttraumatic stress disorder, or social phobia) are needed.

Another common problem is clients' faltering confidence in their ability to overcome a phobia. Clients who have had a specific phobia for many years or whose phobia is very intense often assume that their phobia is part of "their personality" and is therefore unchangeable or would take forever to overcome. At this point, it is worthwhile to provide the general reassurance that these types of treatments are very effective, even for intense fears that have persisted for many years. Furthermore, it is helpful to remind clients that effort is more predictive of treatment efficacy than severity or length of duration and that the client can decide the pace of treatment. Finally, clients may be reminded that it is better to judge a treatment's effectiveness after engaging in the treatment for a while rather than without any evidence from which to judge success.

Chapter 3 | *How Do Phobias Develop?*

(Corresponds to chapter 2 of the workbook)

Outline

- Educate clients about the nature of fears and phobias in general

- Introduce the concept of *prepared fears*

- Discuss the three pathways through which specific fears are acquired

- Explain the factors responsible for the persistence of phobias

  The goals of this chapter are to provide education to enhance the notion of clients' becoming personal scientists of their own emotional reactions and to provide a comprehensive treatment rationale.

Materials Needed

- Fear Acquisition form

The Nature of Fears and Phobias

Overall, the information conveyed in this chapter is intended to disconfirm the common misperception that fears develop from general deficiencies in one's personality or character. Instead, fears are presented as developing and persisting through very specific pathways and mechanisms. Understanding the variables that lead to the onset of phobias and that maintain phobias helps foster the belief that phobias can be explained and treated.

Also, explanations of why certain fears develop, why some people are more vulnerable than others to develop fears, how certain experiences lead to the onset of fears, and why fears persist educate clients about their own reactions in a way that facilitates their developing more objective self-awareness. To become a scientific observer of one's own reactions is a hallmark of cognitive behavioral therapy.

The material in this chapter covers basic experimental concepts relevant to the etiology and persistence of fears: preparedness, traumatic conditioning, vicarious or observational conditioning, informational transmission, avoidance, safety signals, relief, reinforcement, negative cognitions, stress, and physiological and genetic predispositions.

This information helps clients develop a framework for understanding their phobias that is realistic and empirically based and sets the stage for specific steps toward overcoming fearfulness. For example, realizing the role of traumatic conditioning or vicarious observation in the etiology of fears may correct misperceptions of phobias as being indicative of "craziness," "weirdness," or "weakness." Furthermore, information about the factors that contribute to the persistence of fears and phobias (i.e., avoidance behavior and anxious beliefs) provides a rationale for the cognitive therapy (beliefs) and exposure therapy (behaviors) treatment strategies.

The overall message is that fears are likely to develop given the right combination of experiences and individual factors. Furthermore, individual factors (such as genetic factors) do not guarantee the development of specific phobias but rather may predispose the individual to develop a specific phobia.

The factors responsible for the initial development of a specific phobia are not the same as the factors responsible for its persistence or maintenance over time. In other words, once initiated, phobias tend to persist for other reasons. The treatment targets factors responsible for the persistence of phobias. Thus, this chapter emphasizes that treatment proceeds most effectively by targeting current variables rather than by gaining insight into the past.

Another part of education involves explaining to clients that we, as humans, are all more vulnerable to becoming afraid of certain objects or situations over other objects or situations. In particular, objects or situations (e.g., enclosed places, reptiles, high places) that once threatened the survival of the human species are more likely to become feared when they are paired with negative events. These are called *prepared fears*.

Preparedness does not imply inevitability or a guarantee of becoming fearful of things such as the dark, heights, or reptiles. Rather, it suggests that we are more vulnerable to becoming fearful of these objects than of other objects, through the various pathways of fear acquisition described in the next section. Again, this information is intended to help clients realize that they are not "crazy" or "weird" and to facilitate the development of an objective framework for understanding their phobia that facilitates a problem-solving approach to the treatment.

Acquiring Specific Fears

Rachman (1976, 1977) proposed three pathways through which specific fears are acquired: (1) *traumatic conditioning*—in which a negative event (including unexpected panic attacks) is associated with a previously neutral object or situation (especially if the traumatic event was very intense); (2) *vicarious or observational learning*—seeing someone else be hurt or afraid in a situation; and (3) *informational transmission*—being warned of the dangers of specific objects or situations (e.g., by others, in the news, through reading).

To increase clients' objective understanding of their own fears, they are educated about these pathways and then asked to record on the Fear Acquisition form the way in which their own fears were acquired. An example is shown on page 30. A blank copy of the form is included in the workbook, and extra copies are available on the Treatments *ThatWork*™ Web site (http://www.oup.com/us/ttw).

Many clients are unable to recall how they acquired their fear. This is not to be viewed as problematic, as knowing the time of and reason for onset is not required for effective treatment. Thus, reassure clients who cannot remember the reason why they became phobic that the failure to recall is common and will not interfere with treatment progress.

Fear Acquisition

Phobia	Traumatic Experiences	Observational Learning	Informational Transmission
Elevators	Had an unexpected panic attack in the elevator	Watched a movie in which 5 people were trapped in an elevator	My grandmother always told me to get out of elevators as soon as the door opened
Dogs	Was bitten by a large dog	Saw a dog chase my neighbor	Father always told me to stay away from strange dogs
Storms	Drove in a bad storm and almost was in an accident	Saw lightening strike a tree	I read about someone who was struck by lightning
Needles	Fainted during an injection	Saw brother panic during a blood transfusion	The doctor warned me to look away during a blood test

Figure 3.1

Example of Fear Acquisition form

Factors of Vulnerability

Factors that seem to render some people more vulnerable to developing anxiety and fear include stress, physiological or genetic factors (probably a general predisposition to fearfulness rather than inheritance of a specific phobia, although a more-specific genetic vulnerability may apply to phobias of blood, injury, and injections, and especially to the high rate of fainting in this type of phobia), and lack of previous nonfearful experiences with a particular object or situation (i.e., when prior experiences with the to-be-feared object are numerous and positive, one is less likely to develop phobias after a negative experience than someone who did not have the benefit of prior positive experiences). For a detailed and more comprehensive account of how genetic, other biological, and both general and specific learning experiences come together to create a specific phobia, see Antony and Barlow (2002).

This information is intended as a brief overview of the factors that contribute to why, given the same negative experience (such as being bitten by a dog), one individual develops a phobia (such as a dog phobia) and another does not. This idea is not to imply that individuals who develop phobias will always have phobias.

Factors of Persistence

Factors responsible for the persistence of phobias include avoidance behavior, which prevents correction of anxious misconceptions about specific objects or situations or about one's reaction to specific objects or situations; feelings of relief that come from avoidance or escape, which reinforces avoidance behavior; and over-reliance on safety signals (objects or people that help clients manage their phobic stimuli).

Consistent with conditioning theory, the workbook highlights the role of avoidance behavior in contributing to the maintenance of phobias in at least three ways. First, avoidance behavior minimizes the opportunity to learn that whatever it is clients are most worried about happening almost never happens and that they can cope with the phobic stimulus and tolerate their anxiety. Second, avoidance generally lessens distress in the short term, but the relief created by such a reduction in distress reinforces avoidance behavior, making it more likely that clients will continue to avoid the phobic stimulus in the future. Third, safety signals (objects or people) serve as another form of avoidance by interfering with corrective learning and generating dependence upon the safety signal.

Also, tendencies to overestimate the likelihood of danger and magnify the negative outcomes of encounters with feared objects or situations contribute to the persistence of phobias. For example, acrophobics (those afraid of heights) overestimate the danger inherent in heights relative to controls (Menzies & Clarke, 1995). In addition, individuals with specific phobias overestimate the likelihood of negative outcomes in relation to their feared stimuli (e.g., Tomarken, Mineka, & Cook, 1989). Moreover, the intensity of a person's fear of spiders correlates with the strength of their beliefs about harm and coping (Thorpe & Salkovskis, 1995). Di Nardo, Guzy, and Bak (1988) found that expectation of harm was more important than aversive experience in maintaining a fear of dogs. Furthermore, catastrophizing thoughts were the strongest predictor of avoidance behavior in a group of acrophobics (Marshall, Bristol, & Barbaree, 1992). Self-efficacy (or, confidence in one's own ability to accomplish the task of dealing with the phobic situation) also predicts phobic avoidance (Bandura, 1977; Williams, Dooseman, & Kleifield, 1984; Williams, Kinney, & Falbo, 1989; Williams, Turner, & Peer, 1985; Williams & Watson, 1985).

Case Vignettes

Case Vignette 1

C: I remember that when I was a kid my sister and her friends would tease me by locking me in the attic. One time they left me there for hours—they forgot about me. I was screaming and screaming.

T: That sounds like a very traumatic event and was probably an important factor in the development of your current fears of claustrophobic situations. But even more important is how you deal with claustrophobic situations now. For example, the fact that you now believe that you will be stuck in an elevator forever, never to be rescued, and that you prefer to avoid elevators probably maintains your fear of claustrophobic situations that was triggered by your traumatic childhood experience. We cannot go back in time to remove the trauma, but we can change the way you react to elevators now, so that you can overcome your fear.

Case Vignette 2

C: You mentioned that learning to correct anxious thoughts is one of the ways to become less afraid. But I don't see how I can change my thoughts about flying. I mean, it really is dangerous to be so high above the ground. What if the plane crashes? It's certain death.

T: Of course, it's true that most people would die in a plane crash, so, in a sense, your perceptions are accurate. However, where you might be misjudging the danger is your estimate of the likelihood of crashing. There are many events in this world that would be fatal if they were to happen, but the chances of their happening are so small that it is unhelpful to worry about them.

Case Vignette 3

C: My mother, both my sisters, and myself—we are all afraid of lightning and storms. I don't know why. We were never stranded outside in a storm or anything like that. Anyway, I think it must be a genetic thing, and I'm worried that my children will develop the same problem.

T: Phobias often "run in families." But let's think about why that might be. Remember how we talked about the effects of watching someone else become frightened, how easily that kind of observation can lead to you becoming fearful yourself? It is very possible that you or your sisters learned to become fearful of lightning and storms by witnessing your mother's fear. Of course, genetics may play a role, too, but even if you are genetically more likely to become fearful, that does not mean that you can't learn to become less fearful. Also, experiences can be arranged for your own children so that they are less likely to become fearful of storms. For example, observing you become less afraid of storms may protect your children against developing this fear.

Case Vignette 4

C: I have no idea why I am afraid of injections. I just know that every time I have to get a needle, I pass out.

T: It is quite common for people who are phobic of needles and blood to pass out, and as you will see in more detail later, the fainting probably relates to a specific physiological pattern that is unique to individuals with blood and injection phobias. However, the fact that you can't remember how your phobia developed will not interfere with your treatment.

Case Vignette 5

C: I know why I am afraid of heights. It's because I have an inner-ear problem that leads me to feel off balance whenever I look over an edge.

T: Sounds like your physical problem certainly makes heights more difficult for you than for other people. The question is, would you remain fearful of heights if the inner-ear problem were completely corrected, and how is it that the inner-ear problem has resulted in such an intense fear as opposed to a general discomfort when up high? Perhaps the inner-ear problem makes you more likely to feel the physical symptoms of being off balance, which in turn leads you to mistakenly believe the risk of falling is greater. Our goal would be to correct any tendencies to over-judge the likelihood of falling, even with the inner-ear disturbance, so that you can tolerate the feelings without becoming so anxious.

Troubleshooting

A substantial minority of individuals with specific phobias are unable to recall any specific events that may have precipitated their fears, perhaps because the events occurred a long time ago or did not directly precede the onset of the phobia. Reassure clients that knowing the precipitating factors is helpful but not necessary for overcoming fearfulness.

In addition, some individuals may appear to have a general vulnerability to develop fears, as if they are primed to become fearful of almost any specific object or situation at the slightest provocation. This is more likely to be the case among individuals who are chronically anxious in general, and such individuals may express hopelessness at the thought of ever being able to overcome all their fears. In these cases, reassure such individuals that learning to overcome one specific phobia may enhance their self-confidence in general and facilitate their recovery from an array of specific phobias. That is, overcoming anxiety in a single situation generates a sense of mastery that helps them recover from fear in a variety of situations.

Occasionally, clients report that they do not avoid the phobic object or situation, nor do they have anxious beliefs, and yet their fear persists. In other words, the factors believed to maintain the phobia reportedly are not present. In these cases, it is worthwhile to conduct more careful questioning, as avoidance may be present but not obvious (such as driving only in the right lane for a driving phobia, or distracting oneself when in a claustrophobic situation). Similarly, anxious beliefs may be discovered through asking what would happen if clients were stuck in the phobic situation with no way of escaping.

Chapter 4 | *Learning About Your Specific Phobia*

(Corresponds to chapter 3 of the workbook)

Outline

- Introduce the Phobic Objects and Situations form

- Introduce the Bodily Sensations form

- Discuss anxious thoughts

- Introduce the Thought Record form

- Discuss avoidance and coping strategies

- Introduce the Avoidance and Coping Strategies form

- Discuss the importance of self-monitoring, and introduce the Phobic Encounter Record

- Assign homework

Materials Needed

- Phobic Objects and Situations form

- Bodily Sensations form

- Thought Record form

- Avoidance and Coping Strategies form

- Phobic Encounter Record

Phobic Objects and Situations Form

The Phobic Objects and Situations form (shown opposite) lists phobic objects and situations to help clients identify and rank their fears in terms of treatment priority. A blank copy is included in the workbook, and additional copies are available on the Treatments *ThatWork*™ Web site (http://www.oup.com/us/ttw).

Bodily Sensations Form

Sometimes specific phobias involve a combination of (1) anxiety focused on the object or situation and (2) anxiety focused on the physical reactions (e.g., racing heart, shortness of breath, dizziness) to the object or situation. The sample Bodily Sensations form on page 40 is also included in the workbook as a blank form and is available on the Treatments *ThatWork*™ Web site (http://www.oup.com/us/ttw). On this form, clients rate how fearful they are of a number of physical sensations when those sensations occur in the presence of the phobic object or situation. The notion of "fear of fear" stems from the conceptualization and treatment of panic disorder, which is viewed primarily as a fear of the physical sensations of fear or panic (Barlow & Craske, 2000). In contrast to panic disorder, however, the fear of physical sensations in specific phobias is typically constrained to the context of the phobic stimulus, such as a fear of breathlessness only when in closed-in spaces. Fears of physical sensations that generalize beyond the context of external phobic objects or situations are more likely to be a feature of panic disorder. In specific phobias, fear of physical sensations tends to be most characteristic of situational phobias and least characteristic of animal phobias.

Anxious Thoughts

Anxious thoughts contribute to fear and anxiety by generating a perception of danger or threat. Anxious thoughts involve perceived dangers inherent in the object or situation ("The plane will crash"), as well as perceived danger associated with fear reactions to the object or situation ("I will lose control if I become anxious in the plane"). Anxious thoughts

Phobic Objects and Situations

Instructions: Make a check next to each specific object or situation in which you experience fear. Once you've checked each object or situation that frightens you, put those items in order to indicate how important a priority it is for treatment. Your highest-priority item would be ranked 1, your second-priority item would be ranked 2, and so on. Only rank the items that you checked.

Type	Check	Specific Object or Situation	Rank
Animals and Insects	_____	Dogs	_____
	_____	Cats	_____
	_____	Mice	_____
	_____	Birds	_____
	_____	Snakes	_____
	_____	Spiders	_____
	_____	Bugs	_____
	_____	Other animal (_____)	_____
Blood, Injection, or Injury	_X_	Blood	_3_
	_X_	Needles	_2_
	_X_	Doctors/hospitals	_1_
	_____	Dentists	_____
Natural Environment	_____	Heights (e.g., balconies, ladders, bridges, ledges)	_____
	_____	Dark	_____
	_X_	Thunder and lightning	_5_
	_____	Water	_____
Situational	_____	Closed in places (e.g., tunnels, elevators, small rooms, stairwells)	_____
	_____	Driving (e.g., on freeways, city streets, or in poor weather)	_____
	_____	Airplanes	_____
	_____	Trains	_____
Other	_____	Vomiting	_____
	_X_	Choking	_4_
	_____	Other (_____)	_____
	_____	Other (_____)	_____
	_____	Other (_____)	_____
	_____	Other (_____)	_____
	_____	Other (_____)	_____

Figure 4.1

Example of Phobic Objects and Situations form

Bodily Sensations

Instructions: For each item, record a number from 0–100 to indicate how frightened you would be to experience the physical sensation in the presence of the situation or object you fear (0 = no fear; 25 = mild fear; 50 = moderate fear; 75 = strong fear; 100 = as much fear as you can imagine. You can select any number from 0–100). Only rate your *fear of the physical feeling* (rather than fear of the object or situation). For example, if you are not at all afraid of sweating when exposed to a snake (regardless of whether the snake itself terrifies you), your fear rating for sweating would be "0." Note that a separate form should be used for each major phobia that you have (e.g., spiders, heights). Record any comments (e.g., "my fear of dizziness is a 75 when I'm driving, but only 40 when I'm a passenger") in the comments column.

Phobic object or situation: __Driving on the highway_____

Sensation	Fear of Sensation (0–100 scale)	Comments
Racing heart	25	
Shortness of breath	40	
Dizziness, unsteadiness, fainting	65	I am afraid that I will faint and crash the car.
Chest tightness	0	
Trembling or shaking	10	
Sweating	0	
Nausea/abdominal distress	0	
Numbness, tingling feelings	0	
Sense of unreality	20	
Difficulty swallowing or choking sensations	0	
Hot flashes or cold chills	0	
Blurred vision	65	Fear of crashing
Other (specify _____)		

Figure 4.2

Example of Bodily Sensations form

differ not only from person to person in the same situation but within individuals across situations. For example, an individual may have mostly anxious thoughts about perceived danger inherent in the object or situation when driving on the freeways ("Another car will cause me to have an accident") and have mostly anxious thoughts about perceived dangers associated with feeling afraid when flying ("I will lose control and jump out of the plane").

To help them identify their own anxious thoughts, clients are instructed to conduct a behavioral assessment by attempting to confront the feared object or situation. Alternatively, you might ask clients to imagine their feared situation to identify associated anxious thoughts. Clients then record their anxious thoughts on the Thought Record form; a completed example is shown on page 42. A blank Thought Record form is included in the workbook, and blank copies are available for download from the Treatments *ThatWork*™ Web site (http://www.oup.com/us/ttw). The behavioral assessment or imaginal procedure is recommended because thoughts tend to be mood-congruent; therefore, inducing the anxious mood state via actual or imagined confrontation with the feared stimulus will help assess the nature of the anxious thoughts.

The concept of mood-congruency is part of the rationale for behavioral assessments. This becomes important in later chapters when considering why anxious beliefs about phobic objects persist: it is because negative thoughts are more likely to come to mind for the client when he or she is in an anxious or fearful state.

Avoidance and Coping Strategies Form

Examples of avoidance behavior include (1) refusing to confront a situation or escaping from a situation, (2) engaging in excessively protective behavior (e.g., a phobic driver drives only in the slow lane on the freeway, or a person who is afraid of spiders wears thick gardening gloves to go into the basement or the attic), (3) using sedating medications, (4) distracting oneself (e.g., counting, reciting rhymes, imagining oneself elsewhere), and (5) over-relying on safety signals.

Thought Record

Instructions: Complete a separate copy of this form for each relevant fear or phobia.

Phobic object or situation: _Elevators_

Thoughts about the object or situation:

1. The doors may get stuck.

2. The cable may snap.

3. The elevator is old and will break down.

4. The elevator has not been checked and could fail to operate.

5. When the doors open slowly they may not open at all.

6. I will be stuck and no one will ever find me.

7. An earthquake could happen while I'm in the elevator.

Thoughts about the way I feel in the situation:

1. I feel like I can't get enough air so I might stop breathing.

2. I feel so lightheaded that I will faint.

3. I feel so anxious that I might lose control and scream.

4. My urge to get out is so strong that I could hit the doors.

5. People will see that I am anxious and will think I'm weird.

Figure 4.3

Example of Thought Record form

It is generally agreed that using distraction to avoid confronting phobic objects or phobic reactions is counterproductive, whereas using distraction as a tool to demonstrate that one can elect to divert attention away from the phobic object without placing oneself at risk may be effective if done properly. However, given the slippery slope from distraction as a tool for corrective learning to distraction as a form of avoidance, we have elected to advise against distraction throughout this treatment and instead encourage objectively focusing upon all aspects of the phobic stimulus throughout exposure therapy.

Safety signals include objects (e.g., lucky charms) or people (e.g., spouse) that lessen one's anxiety, causing the client to rely on the safety signal in order to face the phobic object or situation. However, like all other forms of avoidance, safety signals interfere with corrective learning. That is, both basic science research and clinical research have shown that safety signals interfere with extinction in the first case and with the effectiveness of exposure therapy in the second case (see Hermans, Craske, Mineka, & Lovibond, in press). This may be because clients attribute the absence of harm to their safety signals (e.g. "I did not lose control of the car because my husband was with me"). Such attributions contribute to the notion that the phobic object is indeed dangerous.

Clients are asked to identify on the Avoidance and Coping Strategies Form the various means of avoidance they use to cope with each phobic object or situation; an example is shown on page 44. There is a blank copy in the workbook, and additional copies are available on the Treatments *ThatWork*™ Web site (http://www.oup.com/us/ttw).

Self-Monitoring Using the Phobic Encounter Record

Self-monitoring entails making ongoing observations of phobic reactions and keeping a record of them to observe changes over time, measure the benefits of treatment, and facilitate the development of an objective observer role.

Ongoing self-monitoring is encouraged in place of relying on retrospective recall because memory tends to be distorted by mood. Distortions in recall (e.g., judging prior encounters with the phobic stimulus as being more negative than they actually were) are likely to contribute to anticipatory anxiety about future experiences with phobic stimuli. Therefore, on-the-spot monitoring is an important part of overcoming any specific phobia. Clients are instructed to use a Phobic Encounter Record each time they encounter their phobic object or situation. An example can be

Avoidance and Coping Strategies

Instructions: Complete a separate copy of this form for each relevant fear or phobia.

Phobic object or situation: _Heights_

Avoidance or Coping Strategy	Examples
Refusing to approach the situation	I won't go higher than the fourth floor of a building.
Escaping from the situation	I'll move away from the edge if I feel anxious.
Distraction	I keep my eyes averted from the edge; I try to keep my mind occupied so I am not so aware of how high I am.
Alcohol/medications/drugs	None.
Excessive protection	Sometimes I'll do some research to see how old a bridge is before I'll consider crossing it.
Safety signals	I prefer to be accompanied.

Figure 4.4

Example of Avoidance and Coping Strategies form

found on page 45. There is a blank copy in the workbook, and, as with all the forms, additional copies are available for download from the Treatments *ThatWork*™ Web site (http://www.oup.com/us/ttw).

A main treatment principle of the MYFP program is the development of an objective awareness of one's reactions instead of a subjective, emotion-focused perspective. The latter tends to be characterized by a sense of being victimized by one's fear, while the former, an objective view, is

Phobic Encounter Record

Instructions: Complete a separate copy of this form each time you encounter your feared object or situation.

Date: _June 7, 2006_   Time: _10:00 p.m._

Situation: _Arrived in New York, in taxi from airport to hotel, drove through a tunnel_

Maximum fear (use a 0–100 point scale): _80_

Main bodily sensations (check)

Racing heart	_X_	Shortness of breath	_X_	Dizziness/unsteadiness	___
Chest tightness	_X_	Nausea	___	Sweating	_X_
Trembling	___	Numbness	___	Choking	___
Hot/cold	___	Sense of unreality	_X_		

Other feelings: _Tense feelings in arms_

Thoughts: _This tunnel is too long. What if the traffic stops or what if the taxi breaks down? It's closing in. I feel as if I can't breathe. I want to jump out of the car and run out of the tunnel—what if I do jump out of the car? I'll die?_

Behavior: _Looked down at my feet and "held on." Held my lucky charm in my hand. Tried to focus on what I had to do as soon as I reached the hotel._

Figure 4.5

Example of Phobic Encounter Record

more likely to foster a sense of mastery and control over one's reaction to phobic cues. These concepts are drawn from pain research, which has found that a problem-solving coping style significantly improves pain management, whereas a wishful-thinking style does not. An objective self-awareness is developed through recording reactions and the components of the fear response (i.e., sensations, thoughts, behaviors) on the spot when encountering phobic stimuli rather than focusing only on the distress (i.e., "how bad it felt").

If clients are successfully avoiding their phobic object, encourage them to practice using the Phobic Encounter Record by imagining themselves facing their phobic stimulus and recording what they would physically experience, their anxious thoughts and their behaviors.

Homework

✎ Client should spend next week recording all instances of phobic encounters on the Phobic Encounter Record.

Case Vignettes

Case Vignette 1

C: What am I supposed to monitor if I am avoiding driving completely?

T: Imagine yourself driving and record your thoughts, feelings, and behaviors on the Phobic Encounter Record.

Case Vignette 2

C: What if I can't identify what it is that goes through my mind? Sometimes all I can think is "not this again," or "when will this end?" Sometimes I just feel sheer terror.

T: For now, ask yourself some key questions, such as, "What is the worst I could see happening?" or "What would happen if I could not escape from this situation?" If you still can't identify specific negative thoughts, don't worry, because we will focus more on how to identify these thoughts next time.

Case Vignette 3

C: I don't experience any of the physical sensations listed on the Phobic Encounter Record. All I feel is a knot in my stomach and an urge to go to the restroom.

T: You may record other symptoms at the bottom of the form. However, the sensations you are describing sound like "nausea or abdominal distress," which is listed on the form.

Case Vignette 4

C: I am worried that monitoring my fears will make me more afraid.

T: Although it may increase your anxiety initially, especially if you typically try to avoid thinking about your phobia, eventually it will become easier.

Case Vignette 5

C: There is no way I can arrange to do a behavioral assessment for my flying phobia.

T: In that case, imagine being in a plane as vividly as you can, and identify what kinds of thoughts go through your mind.

Case Vignette 6

C: I have to deal with my fears of snakes and lizards many times every day because I know they are out in the backyard. Do I have to fill out a self-monitoring form every time I think about going outside?

T: Ideally, you should. It will provide very valuable information that will help us devise the best possible treatment plan.

Clients are often unwilling to complete the ongoing monitoring of encounters with phobic stimuli. Noncompliance can occur for a variety of reasons, including not understanding how to use the forms, not appreciating the importance of self-monitoring, or fearing that monitoring will increase anxiety. Explore clients' reasons for not complying in detail. If clients state that they lack the time or energy to complete the monitoring form, then you might assume that their level of motivation for completing the treatment program is fairly low. In this case, you might suggest that now is not the best time to begin this kind of program. If clients avoid monitoring because they anticipate it will cause an increase in anxiety, recognize and affirm the possibility of their becoming more anxious initially, then reassure them that the anxiety will eventually decrease with continued self-monitoring. Should clients state that they know how they feel and therefore monitoring is not necessary, point out that monitoring provides information in much greater detail, especially for thoughts, feelings, and behaviors that may change from one encounter to the next. Again, the objective nature of self-monitoring should be contrasted with the subjective ways in which clients usually tend to view their anxiety. Furthermore, the monitoring records will provide concrete evidence they can use to assess their progress over time.

Some clients are likely to be unwilling to do a behavioral assessment, even when it is practically feasible. In this case, evaluate the reasons for the unwillingness. Typical reasons include fearfulness, lack of motivation, and lack of trust in the rationale for the assessment. Although it is not absolutely necessary for clients to complete the assessment, even a brief attempt may help them identify some important aspects of their phobic responses of which they may not have previously been aware. Thus, encourage clients to recognize that their attempt at the behavioral assessment is likely to provide very useful information for their treatment, and remind them that they can stop the behavioral assessment whenever they want. Also, be sure that the rationale for the behavioral assessment has been communicated clearly.

Occasionally, clients report that they do not avoid the object of their phobia and do not have any anxious thoughts but are simply afraid. This perception may reflect a lack of self-awareness. Encourage the client to imagine him or herself as close as possible to the phobic stimulus under conditions in which there is no way to escape; such scenarios may facilitate awareness of anxious thoughts. Also, if feasible, observe the client approach the phobic stimulus; you, being more objective, may identify subtle avoidance behaviors of which the client is unaware. Alternatively, encourage clients to conduct their behavioral assessment with a "helper" whose job is to look for subtle avoidance behaviors.

General Principles of Treatment for Specific Phobias

Chapter 5 | *Developing a Treatment Plan*

(Corresponds to chapter 4 of the workbook)

Outline

- Discuss the basic treatment approach for overcoming specific phobias

- Discuss education and cognitive restructuring

- Introduce the concept of exposure therapy

- Assign homework

  As clients begin their own treatment program, they are instructed to follow the guidelines for exposure to phobic objects and situations, using cognitive restructuring as an adjunct to exposure and deliberate induction of physical sensations if they fear bodily sensations associated with their phobia.

Cognitive Restructuring

There are two main components to the treatment described in the MYFP program. The first component is educational information and cognitive restructuring to correct misinformation and misinterpretations of phobic objects, situations, and feared sensations. In addition, cognitive restructuring helps identify and modify anxious, biased thinking patterns. Cognitive restructuring is a management strategy. Described in the earlier sections of this therapist guide, cognitive restructuring has been found effective for certain fears, including claustrophobia, driving phobia, and other phobias in which the individual clearly misperceives the dangers of the situation, his or her reactions to the situation, or both.

The rationale for cognitive therapy as developed by Beck (1993) is that discussing errors in logic and generating alternative ways of thinking can override negative automatic thoughts and beliefs. Patients are first taught to identify and differentiate thoughts. Then they generate alternatives to counter the automatic cognitive distortions by considering the evidence, considering the realistic odds, and thinking of ways of coping with a situation instead of dreading it. Then they practice using the alternative thoughts when approaching the phobic stimulus. The goal is to have these new thoughts automatically triggered by the stimuli that formerly triggered dysfunctional thoughts. Two cognitive errors are emphasized—one having to do with *valence* (catastrophizing) and the other having to do with *risk* (overestimating the risk or jumping to conclusions)—because anxious thinking is usually characterized by such distortions. Furthermore, clients are encouraged to apply the principles of cognitive restructuring to anxious thoughts about both the perceived dangers inherent in the phobic stimulus and those related to their phobic reaction.

Cognitive restructuring is not intended as a direct means to minimize fear, anxiety, or unpleasant symptoms. Instead, cognitive restructuring is intended to correct distorted thinking; eventually fear and anxiety will subside, but their diminution is not the first goal of cognitive therapy.

Exposure Therapy

The most important component of treatment for specific phobias is exposure to the phobic stimulus, combined, if appropriate, with the intentional induction of feared physical sensations in the phobic context. These exposures are conducted in a systematic, controlled manner to increase tolerance of the phobic stimulus, the physical sensations (if appropriate), and the anxiety itself without engaging in subtle or obvious avoidance patterns. Exposure to the feared object or situation is the traditional behavioral method of treatment for specific phobias. Adding exposure to feared bodily sensations is a new approach specific to fear reactions that are compounded by anxiety focused on the fear reaction itself. In the case of specific phobias, this may emerge as an anxiety about dizziness in high places, becoming paralyzed when confronted with feared animals, losing control in a plane or a car, breathlessness in closed-in situations, and so on.

As mentioned in previous chapters, the goal of exposure therapy is not to immediately reduce fear and anxiety but rather to help the client learn something new through exposure. Therefore, exposure is best structured to permit new learning. Clarifying what clients are most worried about as they face their feared objects, situations, and physical sensations, and clarifying the conditions that will best help clients learn that what they are most worried about never or rarely happens and that they can cope with the phobic stimulus and tolerate anxiety are essential for effective exposure.

This approach differs somewhat from the emotional processing (Foa & Kozak, 1986) view of fear reduction, which posited that initial habituation of the physiological response, which produces short-term fear reduction, is a necessary prerequisite for the cognitive shift that produces long-term fear reduction. The cognitive shift was believed to follow from incompatible information that is derived from the exposure experience. In particular, as a result of direct experience over several trials, the individual learns that the stimulus is not necessarily associated with anxiety (since habituation has removed it) and that the risk of harm is lower and the valence is less negative than originally thought. The first part of this model (i.e., the necessity of short-term fear reduction via habituation) thus led to the assumption that exposure therapy is most effective when the client is encouraged to stay in the phobic situation until fear declines.

However, recent research has shown that neither physiological habituation nor the amount of fear reduction *within* an exposure trial is predictive of overall outcome (see Craske & Mystkowski, 2006), and given that self-efficacy through performance accomplishment is predictive of overall phobia reductions (e.g., Williams, 1992) and toleration of fear and anxiety may be a more critical learning experience than the elimination of fear and anxiety (see Eifert & Forsyth, 2005), the focus now is on staying in the phobic situation until the clients learn that what they are most worried about never or rarely happens or they can cope with the phobic stimulus and tolerate the fear and anxiety. Thus, the length of a given exposure trial is not based on fear reduction but on the conditions necessary for new learning, which eventually allays fear and anxiety across trials of exposure. Hence, what may be most essential for a client to learn is that they can tolerate being afraid while driving from one point to another, in which case sustained fear and anxiety would be helpful to the exposure. Essentially, the level of fear or fear reduction *within* a given exposure is no longer considered an index of learning but rather a reflection of performance; learning is best measured by the level of anxiety experienced when the phobic situation is encountered subsequently.

Throughout, the approach to learning emphasizes developing skills. The amount of benefit is believed to depend on the amount of practice.

Homework

✎ Clients are instructed to continue on-the-spot self-monitoring using the Phobic Encounter Record over the next week and to consider the relevance of each treatment component for their own phobia.

Case Vignettes

Case Vignette 1

C: I just don't know what it is that I am really afraid of; the fear is so overwhelming. So, how can I change my thinking if I am not aware of my thinking?

T: Yes, at first it may appear an impossible task. However, you will find that as you become a more careful observer of your own reactions, especially as you continue your monitoring, and we begin zeroing in on specific themes that seem to characterize your responding, what you are thinking about in those situations will become clearer.

Case Vignette 2

C: Are you joking? There is no way that I am ever going to feel comfortable around dogs. Not only do they scare me to death, but I find them repulsive.

T: The point you raise is quite common—people often feel not only fear but also disgust. However, the disgust often subsides as the fear decreases, and strong feelings of disgust don't seem to affect the outcome of treatment overall.

Case Vignette 3

C: I just don't get it. Are you telling me that all I have to do is to get into a plane and then I won't be afraid anymore? After all these years of agonizing before each flight yet still flying, I don't see how more flying will make any difference.

T: Yes, I see your point. Obviously, you have already been conducting your own version of exposure therapy. The problem is probably in the way you have been approaching the task of flying. Last week we discovered that you engage in a lot of subtle avoidance strategies, like relying on alcohol to make the flight easier and sitting only in the front of the plane. In addition, you have a stream of negative thoughts such as, "the plane could crash," "I shouldn't be flying," and "what if I lost control in the plane?" So, although you are indeed confronting the situation, you are using an avoidant and anxious style. We will be using a completely different approach, so that you can fly while being fully aware of what you are doing and realizing the safety of what you are doing.

Case Vignette 4

C: I know that I will faint when I see blood. I always do, so how are we going to deal with that fact when I start practicing going to the doctor?

T: Most people who are phobic of blood have fainting or near-fainting experiences. As you will see when we talk about the treatment in more detail, you will be taught an exercise that is designed to prevent the tendency to faint.

At this juncture clients commonly express extreme anxious apprehension over having to confront the things they fear, or a strong disbelief in the effectiveness of exposure because they previously confronted the object without success. This apprehension is a natural part of the phobia, and clients should be reassured that exposure will proceed at a manageable pace, so that situations that they believe could never be confronted will eventually become manageable. With repeated exposure, "upward generalization" will occur, so that difficult tasks will become easier as a function of success with less-difficult tasks. If the client is concerned about the effectiveness of treatment because of his or her previous negative experiences with exposure to the feared object, the therapist should point out the differences between the ways in which they have conducted exposure in the past and the way in which therapeutic exposure is conducted during treatment.

A second problem may emerge for the person who is not at all fearful of his or her bodily sensations, so that the notion of deliberately inducing physical sensations in the context of the phobic stimulus has no relevance. In this case, the therapist should ensure that fears of bodily sensations are indeed not a part of the phobia (which is very possible, particularly in the case of animal or certain natural-environment phobias) and inform the client that the fear of physical sensations component of the treatment is not relevant for him or her and those sections can be skipped.

Questions sometimes arise about the amount of effort involved. As clients realize that this type of treatment depends on their own efforts and there is no "magic pill" to make the fear go away, they may become apprehensive about beginning treatment. Discussing the ways in which fears are learned and how they are maintained may help the individual realize that, just as learning is involved in the acquisition of fears, learning is involved in their reduction as well. Help clients recognize that the treatment may be tough at times but with perseverance it is very likely to be effective.

Chapter 6   *Changing Thoughts*

(Corresponds to chapter 5 of the workbook)

Outline

- Teach the client about typical distortions in phobic thinking

- Explain the importance of gathering correct information

- Teach ways to change anxious thinking

- Introduce the Changing Phobic Thinking form

Materials Needed

- Changing Phobic Thinking form

Cognitive Restructuring

Cognitive therapy assumes that fear is based on misperceptions and other cognitive processes that can be corrected via conscious reasoning. The MYFP program is influenced in part by Beck's approach to cognitive therapy (Beck, Emery, & Greenberg, 1985), which relies on the notion of *collaborative empiricism,* in which client and therapist work together to identify and label errors in thinking, evaluate the evidence, and generate alternative, more-realistic hypotheses. The MYFP program also encourages clients to make guided discoveries and design behavioral experiments to test the validity of automatic thoughts and assumptions. In this way, real-life exposure becomes a means for testing and modifying beliefs, which is especially beneficial for clients who feel they do not have evidence by which to make more realistic judgments about their phobic object or situation, because they have always used distraction, escape, or avoidance in the past.

The goal of treatment is to recognize thoughts as hypotheses rather than facts. The client, in the role of a personal scientist, is encouraged to gather and examine confirming and disconfirming evidence and to avoid common errors such as confusing thought with action ("Because I have a thought that I could jump off this balcony, then I will jump off this balcony") or thought with fact ("Because I have a thought that the spider is poisonous, then it is poisonous").

The need to evaluate the evidence for perceived danger is essential, given that judgments based purely on emotional reactivity are likely to be inaccurate. High anxiety will generate biases of inflated risk (i.e., jumping to conclusions) and magnify negative valence of events (i.e., catastrophizing). That is, risk inflation and catastrophizing are adaptive responses that promote necessary self-protection in the case of *real* dangers. However, when there is no real danger, anxious thinking patterns generate further unnecessary anxiety.

The process of cognitive restructuring is one of logical analysis, and through repeated rehearsal, the newly formed, more realistic judgments are more likely to become accessible or available at times of heightened anxiety. That is, rehearsing cognitive challenges is believed to strengthen newly developed cognitions that eventually overshadow the old, fearful cognitions.

A basic premise of cognitive therapy in this treatment program is that discomfort can be endured. The therapy encourages clients to perceive that they can cope with difficult situations, although they may prefer that these situations not occur. Importantly, this includes coping not only with the phobic stimulus but also with their own emotions, including anxiety, fear, and disgust.

Throughout this learning process of identifying and challenging negative cognitions, the therapist serves as a coach providing prompts, asking probing questions, posing insightful contrasts, and generally help the client have his or her own insights and restructure his or her beliefs. Although in some cases the therapist must give information directly to fill gaps in knowledge, Socratic questioning is the preferred method of helping the client change his or her beliefs. An example of the Socratic method in therapy is to ask clients what happened the last time they were driving on a freeway, instead of simply telling them that the chance of being involved in a car accident is probably lower than they think. Similarly, therapists might ask how many times clients have suffocated in an elevator to help them realize that their thoughts of suffocation do not match actual experience. In this way, clients become more actively involved in changing their own cognitions. Research in learning and memory has shown that active learning, in which the learner has to provide a response, results in better long-term retention than does passive learning.

Summary of General Principles for Identifying and Challenging Anxious Thoughts

- ▪ Misappraisal of objects or situations as more dangerous than they really are is central to phobic fear and avoidance behavior, even if these misappraisals are not fully conscious.

- ▪ Misappraisal can derive from lack of information or inaccurate information about the feared objects or situations.

- ▪ A model of the contribution of fear of physical sensations to fear of the phobic stimulus explains how the original fear of the phobic stimulus can be magnified by the additional fear of physical reactions to the phobic stimulus. Specifically, the phobic object, when encountered, is misinterpreted as being threatening. This, in turn, generates fear and creates the physical sensations of fear, which, in turn, are misinterpreted as indicating danger (or as interfering with one's ability to deal effectively with the phobic object), thus generating even more fear. Over time, "fear of fear" may become the primary concern when a person is confronted with the phobic stimulus. For clients who are overly anxious about physical reactions (e.g., persons who believe that lightheadedness means they will faint while driving, persons who believe they will have a heart attack if their heart races), providing a more detailed description of the physiology of fear and anxiety and emphasizing the function and protective value of the various physical changes that take place may be beneficial. This information is in the *Mastery of Your Anxiety and Panic, Workbook, Third Edition* (Barlow & Craske, 2000).

- The habitual or automatic nature of phobic thinking is described. Although thoughts are often automatic, automaticity does not contraindicate conscious cognitive challenging. Identifying these thoughts enables one to identify perceived sources of threat. Fear is a reaction to threat, whether it is real or only perceived.

- Typical patterns of distorted thinking that occur during heightened anxiety are described, as are methods of countering those distortions with more-realistic evidence-based thinking. Two main distortions in thinking are *overestimating* (assuming that negative events are more likely to occur than they really are) and *catastrophizing* (blowing the meaning of an event out of proportion and viewing it as unmanageable or intolerable). Reasons that phobic distortions in thinking persist despite evidence disproving them are presented as well. For example, avoidance behavior, misattribution of safety to unnecessary behaviors and safety signals, misattribution to luck, and tendencies to ignore information that does not confirm one's own beliefs may help maintain distortions in thinking.

- The method for countering overestimation is based largely on probability calculations after reviewing all the evidence. Therapists are to use a questioning approach to help clients gain familiarity with a rating scale to reflect realistic probability, where 0 indicates there is no chance the event will happen and 100 indicates the event will definitely occur. This scale can be used to challenge anxious thoughts in a concrete way. For example, a rating of 10 for the probability of falling from a balcony would indicate that the person has fallen 1 out of every 10 times he or she has been on a balcony. In gathering evidence to develop realistic probabilities, the reasons for persistence of distorted logic are examined. Reasons such as "I was lucky" or "It could still happen" suggest emotional reasoning rather than rational responding and should become cues to use a more evidence-based approach.

The method for decatastrophizing is to examine the worst, recognize that adversities are time limited, and generate ways of coping. For example, the client is encouraged to consider what he or she would do to cope if stuck in an elevator (as opposed to considering only the horrific nature of the experience). The therapist also challenges evaluations of the phobic stimulus as being insufferable or intolerable by asking, "So what?" (e.g., "What is so bad about touching a spider?"). The implied message is that although events may be uncomfortable or unpleasant, they can be endured.

The Changing Phobic Thinking form helps clients begin to identify and challenge negative phobic thinking distortions. A blank copy of this form is included in the workbook, and additional copies are available for download from the Treatments *ThatWork*™ Web site (http://www.oup.com/us/ttw). An example of a completed form is provided on page 64.

Case Vignettes

Case Vignette 1

C: If fear is a normal emotion, why does it feel so strange? And why don't other people feel like I do when they drive on the freeway? To feel unreal at the wheel of a car is not normal, and none of my friends feels that way.

T: Even though the emotion of fear is normal, the experience of fear at times when it is not necessary, such as when you are driving on the freeway, may lead you to misperceive the emotion as being abnormal. As we discussed earlier, misperceptions about what it means to become fearful (that is, viewing your fear as a sign of a serious abnormality) may serve only to increase your anxiety about driving. Although your friends may not feel anxious when they are driving, there are probably other situations in which they feel anxious, even though there is no real need for them to feel that way. In fact, your friends could very well experience fear in situations in which you don't feel anxious at all.

Changing Phobic Thinking

Instructions: Each time you experience anxiety or fear in relation to your phobic object or situation, complete this form. In the first column, record the event or situation that triggered your fear. In the second column record your initial fearful predictions and thoughts. In column 3, record realistic alternative thoughts about the situation. In the last column, record the extent to which you believe your initial thought was true, after considering all the evidence (use a 0–100-point scale, where 0 = definitely not true, and 100 = definitely true.

Event	Initial negative thoughts	Alternative outcomes and coping orientation	Realistic probability of initial negative thought coming true (0–100)
Drove through a tunnel	The tunnel might collapse	Tunnels are well built and chance of collapse are minuscule. I will remember that the worst will be that I'll feel anxious.	1%
Spider moved quickly	The spider may get on me.	The spider is probably afraid of me and likely to crawl away from me. Besides, even if it gets on me, the worst thing that will happen is I will feel uncomfortable.	5%
Received a blood test	I may faint.	I know that fainting isn't dangerous. I will regain consciousness in a few seconds.	50%
	The needle will hurt a lot.	I know from past experiences that needles don't hurt much.	5%

Figure 6.1

Example of Changing Phobic Thinking form

C: You know, I realize that the stupid spider will not hurt me. I under-stand all that, and yet I am afraid of it. What's wrong with me?

T: Well, it's very possible that your thoughts are different when you are in the midst of feeling anxious about spiders. Let's examine that possibility. Let's imagine that a spider were suddenly to appear on the arm of your chair. What would be your first thought?

C: I would be very scared, and my first thought would be to get away as quickly as I can, and then I would be worried about embarrassment because here I am—a grown woman who is afraid of a silly spider.

T: So, one thought is self-criticism for not dealing with a situation. Con-tinuing with this type of questioning, let's imagine that, for some rea-son, you can't get away. Instead, you have to deal with the spider by removing it from the chair or whatever. What would you be thinking about?

C: Well, first of all, I wouldn't have a clue what to do. But even if I did, I would be scared to death that somehow it would crawl toward me and even get on my skin.

T: And, what if it were to do that?

C: Well, then I would freak out, just scream, and collapse to the floor.

T: So, how likely is that?

C: Very likely.

T: What tells you that it is very likely that you would freak out, scream, and collapse to the floor?

C: Because I can't imagine it any other way.

T: So, now we have identified another thought that is probably contribut-ing to your anxiety—the thought that you would lose control and col-lapse to the floor. Could that be an overestimation?

C: Well, I'm not so sure. There was that time a few years ago when I really did lose it—I literally ran out of the room screaming.

T: Did you collapse to the floor?

C: No, but I easily could have.

T: What is another way of looking at that? The evidence says that you were very frightened, but you didn't collapse.

C: So, perhaps I just think I could lose it when in fact I will not.

Case Vignette 3

C: Sure, I can tell myself that I'm not going to fall off the balcony. I tell myself that all the time. But what if I did fall?

T: By asking that type of "what if" question, it sounds as it you are dismissing the evidence and reacting emotionally as if it were going to happen.

C: I guess I am, because it certainly feels as if it could happen.

T: Let's check the evidence again. How many times have you fallen off the balcony? Remember, "feeling as if" is not the same as actually falling.

Case Vignette 4

C: It's easy to ask myself these questions now, but I will have no chance of thinking rationally when I am feeling scared.

T: Remember, there is always a reason that you are feeling scared. Fear is a reaction to a perception of danger. So, recognizing what it is you are most worried about is the first step. As with all skills, changing your anxious thoughts takes practice to become effective as a tool. Initially, you may not be able to apply this strategy at the height of your emotion, which is why we begin by discussing these ideas when you are feeling relaxed. But with practice and rehearsal, the skills will become more natural and easier to apply in times of fear.

C: My biggest fear about flying is that I'm trapped. What if I get the feeling of wanting to get out of the plane when it's in flight? I can't tell myself anything to reassure myself, because there is no way out.

T: It is important to identify the underlying thoughts. So, what if you can't get out of the plane—what are you afraid might happen?

C: That's difficult. I don't usually let myself think of that possibility. I think I'm afraid that I'll get so scared that I might lose control and run to the door of the plane and try to open the emergency exit.

T: So, there is a very specific scary image. I think anyone would feel anxious in a plane if they were thinking what you were thinking. So, examine the evidence and judge the realistic probabilities.

C: Well, the last time I tried to take a flight, I made them pull back to the terminal just after they moved onto the runway, so I could get off. So, I would say the probabilities are pretty high.

T: Are you saying that the two situations are the same—pulling back to the terminal from the runway and opening the emergency door in mid-flight? Are there any differences?

C: Well, I think if I could do one thing, then I could do the other as well.

T: What about the possibility that when an escape route is feasible, you will take it—like the terminal runway situation, but when an escape route is not possible, you will tolerate the anxiety?

C: I would like to believe that, but I feel like I am out of control in those situations.

T: Feeling out of control sounds like an interpretation you are placing on the state of being afraid, and remember, being afraid is actually representative of being very much in control. When you were in the plane on the runway, you did what you had to do at the time to get off the plane. Although it reflected unnecessary anxiety, your behavior was very goal-directed—to get off the plane—and suited to the circumstances. Is it possible that you would react differently under different circumstances?

C: So, I should just tell myself not to worry. Even though I am terrified of the lightning and thunder.

T: In a way, that's correct, but it's much more effective to be as specific as you can. Rather than simply telling yourself to be less anxious, identify the specific reasons that you are afraid of the lightning and thunder, and then challenge any distorted predictions. What is it about the lightning and thunder that frightens you?

C: That I will be struck down and die.

T: So, using our 0 to 100 scale of probability, what is the real likelihood of that happening?

C: Maybe it's only 5%.

T: Remember, 5% means 5 times in a 100, or 1 time in 20.

C: Oh, then I suppose it's even less likely than that . . .

Case Vignette 7

C: I can't stand spiders or bugs of any kind. I don't know why, they just gross me out.

T: What do you think would happen if a spider suddenly appeared on the tabletop where you were working?

C: I would freak out. I'd be terrified to move in case it jumped on me.

T: And if it were to crawl onto your body, what then?

C: I can't bear to think about it. It might get under my clothing, and I'd never be able to find it. I would be always thinking that it was on me. I would be looking for bites, and I might end up in a coma during my sleep from the poison of the bite.

T: Now, are any of the thoughts you have just described examples of overestimations?

C: I don't know. It's too difficult to think about logically.

T: Well, starting with the idea of the spider jumping on you. How likely is that to happen? Also, we can examine how likely it would be for you to end up in a coma if a spider were to bite you.

Case Vignette 8

C: I just can't stand to look at them. I get the heebie-jeebies when I think about a spider crawling on me.

T: How would you describe a spider to someone who didn't know what a spider was?

C: A horrible, creepy, poisonous, ugly creature.

T: And what would you tell that same person to do when they found a spider?

C: I don't know, run away, I guess.

T: OK, so now describe a spider and what to do with one as if you were a scientist who studied insects and spiders.

C: I suppose I would describe it as a small, eight-legged creature. I don't know what I would tell them to do if they saw a spider.

T: So, there is a big difference in the way the same thing is described. Considering the objective elements of the spider as opposed to your own dislike of a spider has a big effect. Obviously, knowing what actual steps to take to deal with a spider would help even more in de-catastrophizing your judgments about spiders.

Case Vignette 9

T: One specific self-statement you have identified is that you will suffocate in the elevator. What leads you to think that suffocation is likely to happen?

C: Well, I guess it really feels as if I will.

T: Be more specific. What feelings?

C: Well, I feel like I can't fill up my lungs properly and that I'm gasping for air.

T: And what happens next?

C: Nothing really, except that I can't wait to get out of the elevator, and when I do get out, the feelings subside and I feel as if I can breathe normally again.

T: And how many times have you felt that way?

C: Not very often, because I try to avoid elevators as much as possible. But I force myself to get into an elevator about once every few weeks.

T: So, over the last 12 months, you have felt that way in an elevator at least 12 times?

C: Around about, yes.

T: And how many times have you actually suffocated?

C: Well, none.

T: So, is there another interpretation that is more realistic, based on the evidence to date? Is there another way of interpreting the shortness of breath instead of viewing it as a sign that you will suffocate?

C: I suppose that maybe I'm just not breathing properly, but I really won't suffocate.

T: That sounds more accurate. Now, what percentage would you put on the chances that the next time you get into an elevator you will suffocate?

C: Well, maybe it's only 10%.

T: Now, remember, a 10% chance means that 1 out of every 10 times, you have suffocated.

One issue that sometimes arises when clients are gathering information to fill gaps in their knowledge or correct anxious misconceptions is that they attend selectively to negative information that confirms their already overly negative predictions. For example, a client may read about insects and bugs and find a source of information that says some spiders are fatal to humans. This information may override other, more neutral information that was previously learned (e.g., that most spiders are harmless). To counteract the tendency for selective attention, the therapist should ask clients to find several examples of disconfirming information for every piece that supports their fearful beliefs.

Some clients may hesitate about gathering information because they believe the information will generate more anxiety. They would prefer to know less than more. This is best viewed as an example of avoidance. Hesitation to gather fear-relevant information should be identified as maladaptive, and the client should be encouraged to use a graduated approach, beginning with seeking less difficult or smaller pieces of information. Seeking information is an important step in becoming an objective observer; one should not rely on subjective interpretations of the feared object or situation.

As depicted in one of the vignettes, clients may report that they remain afraid even though they know the chances of danger are slim. By focusing on a recognized slim-chance event, clients are again engaging in overestimation. That is, they have thrown out the realistic probabilities. Remind clients that although it cannot be guaranteed that a particular event will not occur, they are reacting as if the feared outcome is highly likely, despite evidence to the contrary. For example, it is always a possibility that when we cross a street we will be hit by a car. However, most of us are willing to take that risk, because the likelihood of being hit is fairly slim. Another common statement by clients is that they are fully aware of their safety when not anxious, but in the midst of feeling scared, they are convinced that they are in danger. This reflects the state dependency of cognitions. Rehearsal in nonanxious states, however, should have a carryover effect, so that more realistic thoughts will eventually be accessible in anxious times.

Occasionally, clients will say that their worst fear came true, and therefore the chances for future dangers in relation to their feared object or situation are high. For example, the person who is afraid of animals may indeed have been attacked, or the person who is afraid of elevators may indeed have been stuck in an elevator. In these cases, the therapist can continue to point out that the chances of that event happening again remains small and help the client recognize that the event was not as catastrophic as recalled, or both.

As illustrated in case vignette 5, problems occasionally arise because clients view their escape behavior as "out of control." Examples of these "out of control" escape behaviors might include banging the doors to get out of an elevator, requesting that the plane be pulled back to the terminal, and running away from an animal. In each case, the behavior is one of escape, is motivated by fear, and is logically connected with whatever it is the person is most worried about happening. The behavior is an attempt to gain control or to get away from danger and toward safety. In these cases, help the client understand that the actual behavior is motivated by specific anxious beliefs and is designed to achieve a goal, and is therefore not out of control. That is, attention should be directed toward the underlying anxious beliefs that motivated the behavior. Then, remind clients that the MYFP program is designed to eliminate the need to engage in such behaviors. That is, clients will realize that they are at little risk for danger even if they do not escape or do not engage in behaviors that they label "out of control."

A final issue arises for persons whose fear reactions interfere with adaptive coping (e.g., the person who "freezes" in high places; the person who faints at the sight of blood; the person who shakes so much that it is difficult to drive). Reassure clients that these interferences will decrease as they learn new coping skills, increase their self-efficacy, and become less anxious.

Chapter 7   *Preparing for Exposure*

(Corresponds to chapter 6 of the workbook)

Outline

- Help the client understand and prepare for exposure exercises

- Introduce the Exposure Hierarchy form

- Help the client find a helper

- Assign homework

Materials Needed

- Exposure Hierarchy form

In-Vivo Exposure

The purpose of in-vivo exposure is to help clients overcome phobias by learning that whatever it is they are most worried about never or rarely happens and that they can cope with the phobic stimulus and tolerate the anxiety.

Given the specific mechanisms through which exposure is believed to work, there are right ways and wrong ways to conduct in-vivo exposure. Doing it the wrong way probably accounts for the lack of success clients have had previously when they have attempted to expose themselves to fear-provoking situations. The information in this section is intended to demystify in-vivo exposure and elevate its credibility for those whose prior experience has been negative.

Reasons that in-vivo exposure may not have been effective in the past include failure to recognize the differences between difficult or negative one-time experiences and repeated systematic exposure practice; too much time between practices; insufficiently long practices that mitigate corrective learning (i.e., learning that the anticipated negative consequences rarely or never occur or that one can cope with the phobic stimulus and tolerate the anxiety); and subtle avoidance, safety signals, and distraction strategies being used during practices.

The previous chapter outlined the mechanisms proposed to account for fear reduction via exposure therapy. Ongoing investigation reveals the importance of developing self-efficacy, recognizing that whatever it is one is most worried about rarely or never happens, and recognizing that one can cope with the phobic stimulus and tolerate anxiety and other negative emotions. As emphasized in the previous chapter, the level of fear reduction *within* a given exposure trial is less important than achieving the conditions necessary for new learning, regardless of the level of fear. Thus, whereas previous models of exposure therapy emphasized remaining in the phobic situation until fear declined and needing physiological habituation before corrective learning could take place, current models of exposure therapy emphasize remaining in the phobic situation until new learning is acquired, including learning that one can tolerate high levels of fear or discomfort for a designated period of time. Over repetitions of such structured exposures, fear and anxiety eventually decline. Too much emphasis on fear reduction within an exposure trial conflicts with the latest research indicating that fears and anxiety disorders may be partly generated by over-rigid attempts to avoid the emotional experience of fear and anxiety; therefore, toleration of fear and anxiety is a critical learning goal. In general, the principle emphasized throughout the treatment is that exposure and cognitive restructuring serve to develop a new set of nonfearful associations among the stimulus (e.g., height), response (e.g., dizziness), and meaning (e.g., "I will fall"). The new set of associations (e.g., height, dizziness, and "I will not fall") gradually become more salient than the old fearful associations, which, through disuse, are less and less likely to guide emotions. Nonetheless, the old fearful associations are likely to remain intact, and, although dormant immediately after treatment, are vulnerable to reactivation under certain conditions, such as contexts that are salient reminders of when the phobia was first acquired or when a phobic reaction was particularly intense.

Exposure Hierarchy

Clients learn to generate an Exposure Hierarchy and list about 10 tasks for a particular phobia according to parameters (such as size, proximity, and duration) that influence how fearful they become. Clients rate these tasks in terms of anxiety (0–100), listing them from most anxiety-provoking to least anxiety-provoking. A blank copy of the Exposure Hierarchy form is provided in the workbook, and below is an example of a

Exposure Hierarchy

Instructions: In the first column list about 10 situations related to your phobic object or situation, ranging in difficulty from extremely difficult to only mildly difficult. In the second column, rate the extent to which each of these situations would trigger anxiety or fear (0 = no anxiety or fear, 100 = maximum anxiety or fear). List the items in order of difficulty, with the most difficult items listed near the top, and the least difficult items listed near the bottom.

Situations	Anxiety (0–100)
Drive 30 minutes on the highway alone during rush hour	100
Drive 30 minutes on the highway alone in light traffic	90
Drive on busy city streets for 30 minutes alone in rush hour	75
Drive on the highway for 30 minutes with a friend in light traffic	70
Drive on city streets in light traffic with a friend	50
Turn left on a residential street	40
Drive in a residential neighborhood for 30 minutes	40
Pull out of my driveway	30

Figure 7.1

Example of Exposure Hierarchy form

completed form. Clients will refine these hierarchies as they read the chapters for particular phobias in the third section of the workbook.

The Role of the Helper

In most cases you, as the therapist, will assume the role of helper. (Note: It is important that you be sure that you are comfortable in the phobic situation before beginning exposure practices with the client.) It may be useful to involve a client's significant other, family member, or friend in the treatment process as well. There are a number of potential benefits to using a helper:

1. Helpers may assist with gathering phobic stimuli (e.g., spiders) and bringing them to treatment sessions. In addition, they may help identify phobic situations in the client's neighborhood (e.g., pet stores, high places, enclosed places).

2. Including a helper in the initial treatment sessions will help that person become more knowledgeable and therefore more tolerant of the client's phobia.

3. Including a helper will allow the therapist to educate that person about behaviors that may be contributing to avoidance behavior and therefore to the maintenance of the client's phobia (e.g., protecting a client with a snake phobia by changing the television channel whenever a snake appears on the screen).

4. Helpers can act as coaches during exposure practices. Involving significant others may help the client be more compliant with homework practices and stay in the phobic situation for the assigned duration of the exposure task.

5. Helpers can model nonfearful behavior during exposure practices.

It is not absolutely necessary to involve a helper or significant other; the majority of clients improve even when additional help is not available. However, the therapist should consider involving a helper if possible. A helper may be particularly useful for clients who are reluctant to comply with exposure practices and those who need assistance creating the phobic situation (e.g., collecting spiders for individuals with spider phobias, driving for individuals who fear riding in an automobile). If the client has a significant other who is supportive and motivated to help, we recommend that he or she be included.

The significant other or helper can be involved in several ways. First, invite the individual to the initial sessions, during which the treatment rationale and procedures are explained. In addition, suggest that the helper read the workbook. Also, the helper should be present during at least one of the therapist's exposure sessions to see how the therapist behaves during exposure practices and handles problems that arise. During the sessions, encourage the significant other to ask questions to clarify any misunderstandings regarding the information being presented. However, during therapist-assisted exposure sessions, we recommend that the significant other simply observe. Having the therapist and significant other both take an active role during a particular exposure practice will likely be distracting and confusing for the client, particularly if they provide conflicting instructions to the client during the exposure.

The ideal helper should be supportive and unlikely to become frustrated with the client. Exposure sessions may progress very slowly with clients who are particularly phobic. The helper should know when to back down during the practice and remember that it is the client, and not the helper, who must set the pace of the session. In addition, the helper must not have the same phobia as the client. For example, a significant other who has a fear of snakes cannot effectively coach a client with a snake phobia. Similarly, a spouse who is nervous whenever he or she is in the passenger seat of the client's car would be detrimental to a client with a driving phobia. The helper must be willing and able to model nonfearful behavior during practices. A helper who is fearful may actually increase the client's fear.

The helper should be someone who can accept the client's discomfort. For example, clients may cry, scream, or even vomit upon exposure to the phobic situation. Individuals with blood phobia may faint during exposure sessions. The helper must be able to tolerate these responses and still be supportive and encourage the client to complete the assigned exposure practice and to manage the associated anxiety. The helper should not become angry or overly worried by these responses. Rather, he or she should be able to accept the client's discomfort as a normal part of overcoming the phobia.

Homework

✎ Complete Exposure Hierarchy form

Case Vignettes

Case Vignette 1

C: There is no way I will ever be able to sit in a dentist's chair to have my teeth cleaned, let alone endure the time it takes to have cavities filled.

T: As you move step-by-step up your hierarchy, beginning with sitting in the waiting room, then sitting in the dental chair for a few minutes, then sitting in the dental chair for a brief examination, and so on, each new step will become easier than you originally thought because of your success with the earlier steps.

Case Vignette 2

C: Surely there is more to this than just practice. I mean, doesn't my fear reflect some deeper underlying conflict or issues? Don't we need to find out what is really bothering me in order to overcome my fear?

T: Although it is possible that your fear was precipitated by a particular concern or conflict in your life, we know that the most effective way of overcoming fears is to repeatedly confront the object over and over again, so that you learn to be less fearful.

C: I am afraid of so many places—how can I possibly get around to practicing all of them?

T: Experiences that you have in one situation should carry over to similar situations. Learning not to be afraid in one situation should make it easier for you in other similar situations.

Troubleshooting

Clients typically express anxiety in anticipation of the in-vivo exposure; this may become apparent in a variety of ways. For example, they might make direct statements of anxious apprehension, question the credibility of exposure, or procrastinate about getting started with in-vivo exposure. Recognizing that exposure takes some courage but is rarely as difficult as expected is helpful. Indeed, research has shown that the level of anxiety experienced when anticipating exposure is often stronger than the level of anxiety felt during exposure; in other words, clients most often overestimate their level of anxiety. Using a graduated approach to exposure and incorporating the new information and cognitive strategies helps exposure practices seem less threatening.

Sometimes clients are unsure why they doubt the value of exposure. Having them describe a recent phobic experience and provide specific details may point to differences between these attempts and therapeutic exposure practices. Clients who continue to doubt can simply be asked to attempt the program despite their doubts, given the empirical support for exposure-based treatments, and to forestall their judgments until they have some experience with the exposure treatment program.

A more practical issue concerns the construction of the hierarchy. Of course, the hierarchy is phobia-specific, meaning that a different hierarchy should be constructed for each different phobia. Within a phobia, there might be a variety of factors that determine the level of fear experienced, such as size of the object, proximity of the object, length of time with the object, and so on. For the purpose of this program, all the relevant parameters are mixed in one hierarchy. However, it is also possible to create more than one hierarchy for each phobia, with each hierarchy representing one parameter. For example, a fear of driving may be a function of (1) how long the drive takes, (2) whether a highway or surface streets are used, and (3) whether one drives in inside or outside lanes. A separate hierarchy could be created for each of the three dimensions.

Sometimes it is difficult to develop a hierarchy because everything related to the phobia seems intensely anxiety-provoking—that is, the least anxiety-provoking situations do not differ greatly from the most anxiety-provoking ones. For example, flying in a small plane may be as distressing as flying in a large plane. In these cases, you may initially add safety signals (e.g., being accompanied, sitting at the front of the plane) to generate items that produce less anxiety. Of course, the goal is to eventually eliminate reliance on safety signals.

Similarly, the person who has avoided the phobic object or situation for a long time may have difficulty creating the hierarchy. Usually, imaginal exposure can assist these clients. Finally, it is important to remember that the hierarchy developed at the onset of the program can be adjusted as necessary throughout treatment.

Chapter 8   *Specifics of Exposure*

(Corresponds to chapter 7 of the workbook)

Outline

▣ Discuss details of conducting real-life exposure therapy

▣ Discuss ways of deliberately inducing physical sensations during exposure

▣ Introduce Exposure Rating form

Materials Needed

▣ Exposure Rating form

Details of Conducting In-Vivo Exposure

The material in this chapter follows directly from the previous chapters describing the mechanisms of exposure. Exposures are to be conducted for long enough or enough times to permit corrective learning; they must (eventually) be conducted without distractions, subtle avoidances, or safety signals, all of which interfere with corrective learning. The corrective learning pertains to learning that whatever one is most worried about never or rarely happens or that one can cope with the phobic stimulus and tolerate fear and anxiety. Recent research suggests that fear reduction within any particular exposure trial is not related to fear reduction over the long term. Therefore, the duration of a given exposure trial is not based on how long it takes for fear to decrease but rather on a predetermined length or number of trials at which clients will most effectively learn something new. For example, if clients believe with certainty that they will fall from a height if they stand there for 10 minutes, but not for 5 minutes, then the most effective exposure will be for 10 minutes. Similarly, if clients believe they can tolerate the anxiety associated with driving on the freeway once (but not five times) on a particular day, then the most effective exposure will be to drive five times.

As described earlier, fear can be triggered by *exteroceptive cues* (e.g., an object or situation), *interoceptive cues* (e.g., internal physical sensations), or a combination. Panic disorder is primarily a fear of interoceptive cues, whereas agoraphobia and some specific phobias seem to represent a combination of interoceptive cues and exteroceptive situations, and other specific phobias (such as animal phobias) seem to be largely exteroceptively cued. Nevertheless, individual differences exist such that some people with animal phobias are fearful not only of a specific animal but also of a physical sensation that occurs when they are frightened by an animal.

Managing fear of physical sensations in the context of phobic objects or situations involves corrective information (as discussed in previous chapters), cognitive restructuring for misinterpretations of the physical sensations, and direct experience with the physical sensations to learn they are harmless.

The cognitive techniques discussed previously are incorporated as anxiety-management strategies to be used in conjunction with real-life exposure practices.

The exposure procedures are described as they would be conducted by the client without the aid of the therapist. However, the therapist can be included in some early stages of exposure, particularly to model mastery behaviors, provide feedback to correct maladaptive protective behaviors, maintain control over the situation (e.g., controlling a feared animal), or serve as a safety signal when the client is too anxious to perform the task on his or her own. Eventually, however, as with all safety signals, the therapist should be removed, perhaps gradually with the aid of telephone calls, so that the client achieves full self-mastery.

Number of practices. Clients should repeatedly practice an item from the exposure hierarchy until they have truly learned that what they were most worried about rarely or never happens or that they can cope with the phobic stimulus and with being anxious in that situation. Therefore, the number of practices will differ from item to item and person to person.

Duration of exposure. One long, continuous practice is usually more effective than short, interrupted practices because more corrective learning is possible with lengthier practices. In general, the length of the exposure should be long enough (or repeated enough times) for clients to learn that whatever they are most worried about does not happen or that they can cope with the phobic stimulus and with their anxiety.

Massed versus spaced exposure. Exposure works best if practices are scheduled close together. Clients should practice exposure at least three times a week, with at least one day off a week.

Graduated versus intense practices of exposure. Clients should progress as fast as they are willing to go and eventually practice the most anxiety-provoking item on the hierarchy.

Controlled escape. If clients feel overwhelmed, they may briefly escape from an exposure trial but should always return to complete the exposure task on the same day.

Avoidance, safety signals, and distraction. Clients are encouraged to eventually complete exposure practices without the aid of subtle means of avoidance, safety signals, or distraction.

Knowing what to expect. Clients are told to expect some discomfort when the exposure is very intense.

Imaginal versus real-life exposure. Real-life exposure is the preferred method, although imaginal exposure may be used when repeated real-life exposures are impractical, fear is extremely intense, or imaginal exposure produces as much fearfulness as does real-life exposure. The workbook also explains disadvantages of imaginal exposure.

- *Deliberately inducing physical sensations.* For those clients whose fear of the phobic stimulus is compounded by fears of their own physical reactions to the phobic stimulus, exposure to the phobic stimulus can be combined with exercises to deliberately induce the feared physical sensations, again to learn that whatever it is that worries them most about the phobic stimulus and about their own physical reactions rarely or never happens and that they can cope with the anxiety associated with both the phobic stimulus and the sensations.

  Below is a list of exercises that your client can use to induce feared physical sensations while confronting phobic objects or situations:

  1. Drive with the heater on and windows rolled up (heat).
  2. Wear wool clothes, jackets, or turtlenecks (heat) when using elevators.
  3. Turn his or her head quickly (dizziness, lack of balance) when on a high balcony.
  4. Hold his or her breath (shortness of breath) when in an elevator or other enclosed place.
  5. Take a few fast and deep breaths (breathlessness, tingling, lightheadedness) when in an elevator or other enclosed place.
  6. Drink a cup of coffee (agitation or racing heart) for any phobic situation.

- *Integrating cognitive restructuring and real-life exposure.* Prepare for an exposure practice by helping the client evaluate his or her anxious predictions; ask key questions during exposure to facilitate challenges to anxious thinking and to evaluate progress after the practice.

Using the Exposure Rating Form

Following each exposure practice, the client should complete the Exposure Rating form to track his or her progress. An example of a completed copy is shown below. A blank copy is included in the workbook, and extra copies are available for download from the Treatments *ThatWork*™ Web site (http://www.oup.com/us/ttw).

Exposure Rating

Instructions: This form should be used each time you complete an exposure practice. In column 1, record the date. In column 2, describe the exposure practice (e.g., what did you do?). In column 3, record the practice number (e.g., if this was the second time you practiced that item, you would write "2"). In the last column, record the maximum level of anxiety or fear you experienced, using a scale from 0–100 (0 = no fear; 100 = maximum fear).

Date	Exposure description	Practice number	Maximum anxiety (0–100)
10/5/06	Look at photo of a snake for 30 minutes	1	100
10/6/06	Look at photo of a snake for 45 minutes	2	40
10/7/06	Sit 3 feet from a snake in an aquarium	1	75
10/09/06	Sit 1 foot from a live snake in an aquarium	1	65
10/11/06	Sit 3 feet from a live snake being held by a friend	1	100
10/12/06	Sit 1 foot from a live snake being held by a friend	1	50
10/13/06	Practice touching a snake for 30 minutes	1	85
10/15/06	Practice touching snake for 45 minutes	2	40
10/16/06	Hold a snake for 45 minutes	1	60

Figure 8.1

Example of Exposure Rating form

In general, gains tend to be maintained for long periods following treatment (Öst, 1996b). However, several variables may lead to a return of fear. First, fear may return if there has been a long interval since the last encounter with the phobic object or situation. For example, an individual who overcomes a fear of flying and does not fly again for many years may become fearful during a future flight. Second, a person might reexperience fear if he or she encounters a situation that is more challenging than those practiced during treatment. A height-phobic individual who overcomes the phobia by exposure to balconies, escalators, and other high places encountered in daily life might still experience fear on a trip to the Grand Canyon. Third, fear may be reexperienced if the phobic stimulus is encountered in a particularly salient context, such as one similar to the context in which the phobia was first acquired or one in which a particularly intense phobic reaction occurred. For example, if the fear of driving followed an unexpected panic attack when driving while recovering from an illness, then illness may reactivate the old fearful memories of driving in the future. Fourth, a traumatic experience in the feared situation may lead to an increase in fear. For example, an individual who has a car accident after overcoming a phobia of driving may see the fear return. Finally, general stresses may cause the fear to return. For example, a person who overcame a fear of injections might notice slightly more fear when experiencing heightened levels of general stress (e.g., unemployment, marital difficulties).

Going beyond what might be normally expected is one method of protecting the client from a return of fear. In fact, exposure practices should go beyond what most individuals would feel comfortable doing. For example, people with spider phobias should be exposed to holding and touching harmless spiders, even though most people might not feel comfortable doing so.

Second, individuals should continue to engage in occasional exposure practices whenever the opportunity arises. For example, an individual with a height phobia should purposely look out windows in high buildings whenever possible. A person who has overcome a phobia of dogs should purposely touch friends' dogs whenever possible.

Third, there is some preliminary evidence to suggest that practice in as many different contexts as possible, especially contexts associated with initial phobia acquisition or a particularly intense phobic reaction, might offset the return of fear.

Although fear typically does not return, a person who does experience a return of fear should be encouraged to begin exposure practices as soon as possible. In general, the fear will be much easier to overcome the second time around.

Case Vignettes

Case Vignette 1

C: I can't decide whether to go at this gradually or start with the hardest thing and get it over and done with. What if I make a mistake and choose the wrong approach?

T: Some of this will be learning from your experience. There will be little harm from starting with one approach and then shifting to another approach. Perhaps you can start off a bit more gradually, see how it goes, and speed up as you go.

Case Vignette 2

C: In the past, I have taken a tranquilizer every time I had to fly. Can I still do that?

T: Tell me more about why you have used the tranquilizer.

C: Well, it just helps me get through the flight. I feel that I can make it.

T: And if you did not have the medication available, what do you think could happen in the plane?

C: Oh, the usual—that I would get so anxious that my heart would speed up and I'd end up having a heart attack.

T: So now let's use some of the cognitive skills you have been working on to question that assumption. OK, realizing that it is very unlikely for you to suffer from a heart attack even when the medication is not available is the first step. The next step is to build into your exposure program a way of gradually decreasing the reliance on medications. Perhaps you could start with the medication, then take less of it on the next flight, then just carry it with you on the next flight, and eventually fly without any medication.

Case Vignette 3

C: I think that as long as I can look at snakes I'll be OK. I really don't think it's necessary for me to touch the snake.

T: Of course, how far you go in the end is up to you, but I will encourage you to go further than just looking at the snake, for two reasons. First, knowing that you can handle a snake will significantly boost your self-confidence and sense of mastery in the situation. Second, research has shown that becoming very comfortable with phobic objects, instead of achieving just the absolute minimum, seems to decrease the risk of relapse.

Case Vignette 4

C: What if I really do fall over the edge? I'm not sure this is safe. My legs get so wobbly that I could very well fall over.

T: I understand your concerns, but let's consider whether your concerns are realistic. This will be a good exercise in using cognitive restructuring in rehearsal for your exposure. Now, you are saying that you think you might fall over, and it's the wobbly feeling in your legs that makes you think you could fall. Describe your thinking more.

C: Yes, it's a very strong feeling. Like I have no control over my legs.

T: OK, now is it possible that you are confusing the feeling of weakness with a loss of control?

C: It's possible, but how will I know?

T: Well, how many times have you felt that way, and how many times have you fallen?

C: I have felt that way every time I'm on a balcony, and no, I have never fallen, but only because I have kept away from the edge.

T: Do you think that by setting up very gradual exposure practices so that you start with just a few seconds looking over the rail and gradually increase to minutes, you can gather information to help you realize that you will not fall?

Case Vignette 5

C: Can we do it all imaginally?

T: Why?

C: Because then I wouldn't have to face it.

T: Sometimes imaginal exposure is sufficient, but I would encourage you to eventually practice confronting the situation, for a couple of reasons. First, the reason you prefer imaginal exposure is fear-based, and that in and of itself suggests the importance of eventually confronting the object. Second, imaginal work can be helpful, but being able to imagine an object without fear does not always generalize to real-life encounters. Nevertheless, we can start off imaginally.

Case Vignette 6

C: You said it was important to concentrate on the physical feelings. Does that mean I should concentrate on how awful I feel?

T: The point is not to concentrate on feeling awful but to allow yourself to fully experience the sensations. By giving yourself permission to feel those sensations, you are giving yourself a chance to learn from the experience, to learn that the sensations are not dangerous, and to discover that you can manage despite feeling these sensations.

C: I don't want to deliberately bring on these physical sensations. They scare me. Why should I have to make myself feel these things if they are unnatural in the first place?

T: The fact that you are scared of the sensations is a very good reason for facing them because your fear of the sensations is probably contributing to the fear you experience when you drive on the freeways.

Troubleshooting

As the client prepares for in-vivo exposure, it is important that the previous cognitive skills be fully incorporated every step of the way. Clients might tend to want to rush into exposure therapy, almost blindly, and hope for a good outcome. However, as described, the process of exposure therapy is one of very conscious planning and learning through direct experience. Therefore, the analysis of cognitions before, during, and after each exposure task is important.

As noted in the preceding chapter, clients may express considerable anticipation as they get closer to conducting actual exposure. Reassuring them about the typical course of anxiety and including more-graduated methods of exposure are helpful in these cases.

As alluded to in a case vignette, combining anxiolytic medications and exposure therapy is sometimes difficult, and the research is lacking in this area. However, several theorists have suggested that typical tranquilizers, such as diazepam and alprazolam, interfere with fear reduction during exposure in several ways (Başoğlu, Marks, Kiliç, Brewin, & Swinson, 1994; Bouton & Swartzentruber, 1991). First, clients attribute their success to the medication rather than the self, leading to a psychological dependency on the medication. Second, when clients assume that the medications prevent the feared misperceptions and catastrophes from happening, it interferes with full cognitive restructuring. Third, medications may interfere with full conscious awareness and attention to the experience.

Deliberately inducing the physical sensations in the phobic context may be strongly resisted. In this case, a gradual approach may be helpful. That is, exposure could begin with exposure to the phobic stimulus without purposefully inducing the feared physical sensations. Then, exposure to the phobic stimulus can proceed, with the client directed to fully focus attention of the accompanying sensations. Finally, exposure to the phobic stimulus can be combined with deliberate inductions of the feared physical sensations.

Strategies and Ideas for Various Specific Phobias

Chapter 9 | *General Issues Relating to Chapters 8 Through 14 of the Workbook*

How to Use Chapters 8 Through 14 of the Workbook

Each of the chapters in the third part of *Mastering Your Fears and Phobias* discusses a particular specific phobia and provides more detailed information on the definition, epidemiology, etiology, assessment, and treatment of the phobia. Chapters 8–14 cover:

- phobias of blood, needles, doctors, or dentists (chapter 8)

- claustrophobia (chapter 9)

- animal and insect phobias (chapter 10)

- height phobia (chapter 11)

- driving phobia (chapter 12)

- flying phobia (chapter 13)

- phobias of storms, water, choking, or vomiting (chapter 14)

Each chapter describes specific strategies for adapting the treatment techniques introduced earlier in the workbook for the relevant specific phobias.

Clients should read chapters 1–7 first, before reading the chapter relevant to their specific phobia. The chapters in the third part refer to sections of the first two parts, so it is important that clients be familiar with the material in the first two parts of the workbook before beginning the chapters in the final section.

Occasionally, it may be difficult to determine which chapter is most relevant for a given client. For example, consider the following example of a client who sought treatment for a fear of flying. The client was a 45-

year-old physician who was leaving to attend a conference overseas and was anxious about flying on a small commuter airplane from Albany, New York, to New York City, where he was to transfer to a larger aircraft for his flight to London. Interestingly, he had little fear of the flight to London and was more afraid of flying from Albany to New York City. The following case vignette illustrates a strategy for determining the appropriate diagnosis.

C: I have to fly to London in two weeks and I am absolutely terrified about the first leg of my flight, from Albany to New York City.

T: What frightens you, specifically?

C: Well, the flight from Albany is on one of those tiny planes, and I just don't feel safe on small planes.

T: Does the second part of your trip, on the large plane, frighten you at all?

C: Not really. I'm flying business class, so there will be lots of room.

T: Exactly what bothers you about flying on the small plane?

C: In small airplanes, I feel like I can't breathe. I turn on the air vent, and that helps a bit. It's not as bad when there is no one sitting beside me.

T: Do you worry that the plane might crash?

C: Not really. I know that flying is safe. It's more how I feel on the plane that frightens me. I just get so panicky that I think I might suffocate.

T: Do you ever panic in other situations, or do you sometimes panic for no real reason, just out of the blue?

C: I never panic out of the blue, but I do panic in certain other situations. When the elevator at work is very crowded, I feel like I can't breathe. In fact, last month, I actually had to get off the elevator and wait for the next one. I think that's about it.

T: Are you sure? Let me list some other situations for you. Do any of these bother you? What about being in small rooms with no windows? Tunnels? Lying in bed with the blankets over your head? Sitting in the back seat of a two-door car?

C: Now that you mention it, I'm nervous in most of those situations. I guess they don't come up that often, so I had forgotten about them. In fact, I remember when I first started working, I had to switch offices because mine had no window.

T: Are there other aspects of being on a plane that bother you? For example, does it bother you to be so high in the air?

C: No. Heights don't bother me. I think it's just the closed-in feeling that bothers me. On a small plane it feels like there is no room to move. It's hard to breathe.

The client in this vignette is suffering from claustrophobia. The therapist's questions were chosen to rule out other diagnoses (e.g., flying phobia, height phobia, panic disorder). For this client, the relevant chapter in the third part would be chapter 9 (claustrophobia). The client might benefit from the chapter on flying phobia as well, but it is likely that the chapter on claustrophobia would be most helpful.

In many cases, clients will report fearing a situation for more than one reason. For example, it is not unusual for an individual who fears bridges to have concerns related to their competence as a driver as well as concerns about being up high. For such an individual, we recommend that each relevant chapter in the third part (e.g., driving phobias and height phobias) be read. It is likely that each chapter will contain suggestions helpful to such clients.

Structure of Workbook Chapters 8 Through 14

Each chapter in the third part of the workbook follows the same basic format. The chapters begin with a section to help the client determine whether the chapter is appropriate for his or her phobia. Next is a description and definition of the phobia, along with a case example. Brief reviews of the latest findings on the epidemiology and etiology of the specific phobia are also included.

A step-by-step description shows clients how to apply the treatment strategies from the first two parts of the workbook to their own specific phobia. Clients are taught to identify the specific variables that influence their fear in addition to the specific objects and situations that trigger their fear. Comprehensive lists illustrate some of the relevant variables, and clients are encouraged to generate similar lists for their own phobias. The chapters give examples of typical anxious thoughts and behaviors, and clients identify their own anxious thoughts and avoidance behaviors.

The next step described in each chapter is how to prepare for exposure practices. Clients may incorporate a coach or helper to aid in arranging and conducting practices. Because clients may be unable to approach the phobic object initially, a helper may be essential early in treatment. Of course, the role of helper will most likely be assumed by the therapist, although significant others, family members, and friends may assist during between-session practices. In addition, clients are given strategies for arranging exposure practices (e.g., locating phobic objects and situations).

After clients are prepared for their exposures with the phobic situation, each chapter discusses specific strategies for *implementing* some of the techniques covered earlier in the workbook, including cognitive restructuring, and, if appropriate, exposure to feared sensations. Finally, each chapter in the third part of the workbook closes with a troubleshooting section to help solve problems that might arise during treatment.

In addition to this basic structure, the chapters contain sections on techniques that are uniquely relevant for particular specific phobias. For example, chapter 8 includes a section on how to use "applied tension" to prevent fainting, which is typically associated with blood and injection phobias. Likewise, chapter 12 has a section to help clients assess their driving skills, because deficits in driving skills may be related to fear of driving. Finally, chapter 14 discusses the use of imaginal exposure for treating phobias in which it is impractical to consider in-vivo exposure.

Summary of Steps for Treating Specific Phobias

1. *Making a diagnosis and general assessment.* The therapist should first confirm the diagnosis of specific phobia and rule out other possible diagnoses. In addition, it is often helpful to know the history and course of the phobia.

2. *Determining the parameters of the phobia.* A functional analysis of the client's fear should be conducted to help design the most effective treatment. This part of the assessment should include listing in detail the situations that the individual fears and avoids, specific anxious thoughts, variables that moderate the person's fear (e.g., distance from the object, presence of another individual), and methods of avoidance (including subtle strategies such as avoidance or alcohol use). Examples are included in each chapter in part III of the workbook.

3. *Using the Behavioral Approach Test (BAT).* The BAT is a useful tool for assessing fear in the phobic situation. The client should be encouraged to get as close as possible to the feared object or situation. During the assessment, a variety of parameters can be measured, including fear ratings that use a numeric scale (e.g., 0–100), distance from the phobic object, heart rate, anxious thoughts, and subtle avoidance strategies. If it is not practical to create the feared situation (e.g., for a fear of flying) or if a client refuses to approach the object or situation, the BAT may be conducted in the imagination.

4. *Providing information about the specific phobia.* Before beginning treatment, provide the client with information about his or her specific phobia (e.g., prevalence, possible causes). In addition, provide information to correct misinformation regarding the nature of the feared object or situation. During this discussion, describe the survival value of fear and explain the purpose of the various physical sensations experienced when one is fearful. Emphasize the role of anxious thoughts, expectations, beliefs, and predictions, in addition to the tendency for individuals with phobias to differentially seek out information that confirms their phobic beliefs (e.g., reading about plane crashes). Finally, explain in detail the role of avoidance (including subtle avoidance strategies and safety signals) in maintaining fear and causing further avoidance.

5. *Setting the stage for treatment.* Give clients a treatment rationale in which the treatment is described in detail and the relationship between the treatment components and the variables that help maintain fear (e.g., avoidance, anxious beliefs) is highlighted. In addition,

instruct the client to generate a detailed exposure hierarchy. They should read the relevant sections of the workbook at this point.

6. *Treating the phobia.* Treatment will primarily involve exposure to the feared situation or object. As much as possible, model or demonstrate the exposure task for the client before asking the client to attempt particular steps. Involve a helper who can coach the client during exposure practices. Let the pace of exposure be determined by the rate at which clients are willing to progress to the next step of their hierarchy. Incorporate other strategies (e.g., cognitive restructuring, education, applied tension, deliberate induction of feared physical sensations) into the treatment when relevant. Progress up the hierarchy. Treatment may last as little as one session or as many as 10, depending on the type of phobia. In our experience, animal phobias, blood phobias, and injection phobias often take fewer sessions, whereas height phobias and situational phobias (e.g., driving) typically take more treatment sessions.

7. *Assigning homework.* Instruct clients to practice exposure outside the therapy sessions. In general, exercises to be assigned for homework should first be attempted in the session, with the therapist present.

8. *Assessing progress.* Continue assessment throughout treatment and repeat the BAT periodically to monitor progress. In addition to the BAT, a range of self-report scales are available for assessing particular specific phobias (for a review, see Antony, 2001).

9. *Terminating treatment.* Provide clients with the previously discussed instructions for preventing relapses.

Chapter 10

Overcoming Phobias of Blood,
Needles, Doctors, and Dentists

(Corresponds to chapter 8 of the workbook)

Outline

- Discuss the nature of blood, injection, and injury phobias

- Instruct the client to identify fear triggers, anxious thoughts, and anxious behaviors

- Teach the client how to prevent fainting

- Discuss ways to find the items needed for exposure exercises

- Instruct the client to challenge anxious thoughts

- Remind the client of strategies for exposure exercises

Nature of Blood, Injection, and Medical Phobias

This chapter begins with an introduction to the nature of blood, injection, and injury phobias. These phobias are defined and an evolutionary perspective is used to explain the diphasic physiological response and the tendency to faint that is associated with these phobias and *not* with other phobias. Clients are given a case example and information regarding the epidemiology and etiology of these phobias.

Identifying Fear Triggers and Anxious Thoughts and Behaviors

The initial step in the treatment of blood, injection, and medical phobias is a detailed functional analysis of the client's fear. Specifically, clients are instructed to identify specific phobic cues in addition to the variables that influence the intensity of their fear when confronting the phobic stimulus. Clients are taught to identify their anxious thoughts and the ways in which they avoid situations involving blood, needles, dentists, and related situations. The workbook contains exhaustive lists of typical phobic cues, thoughts, and behaviors to help clients identify these variables for their own phobias.

Applied Tension to Prevent Fainting

A series of instructions on the strategy of applied tension teaches clients who faint in the phobic situation how to prevent fainting. Applied tension temporarily raises blood pressure and thereby interrupts the diphasic response typically associated with blood and injection phobias.

Clients are encouraged to consult a physician before engaging in exposure practices. First, the client should be sure that fainting will not pose any threat to his or her health. Second, a physician can help arrange exposure opportunities by ordering blood draws and giving injections.

Finding Items Needed for Exposure Exercises

The "Finding the Items Needed for Exposure" section in the workbook helps clients locate the objects and situations needed for exposure practices. The section includes suggestions for finding photographs and videotaped scenes depicting blood, injections, and medical procedures. Additional suggestions help the client find real-life situations in which they can see blood or receive injections and minor dental or medical procedures.

Challenging Anxious Thoughts

Clients are instructed to change anxious thoughts by seeking out corrective information and by identifying and challenging probability overestimations and catastrophic thinking patterns. For probability overestimations, clients are expected to look at all the evidence and consider the realistic odds for whatever it is they are most worried about in relation to the phobic stimulus and, where appropriate, in relation to the physical sensations they experience in the context of the phobic stimulus. For catastrophizing, clients are expected to face the worst and realize that it is not as bad as first thought and to focus on ways of coping. Decatastrophizing is particularly suitable for worries about not being able to tolerate fear or other emotions such as disgust.

Exposure-Based Strategies

Remind your client of specific strategies for conducting exposure practices, such as ensuring that sessions are constructed to permit the client to learn that whatever he or she is most worried about rarely or never happens or that he or she can cope with the phobic stimulus and accompanying anxiety. Practices should be frequent, planned, and challenging. Clients are informed that for exposure to be beneficial, they will most likely need to experience discomfort during the practice sessions, especially since a critical learning experience is the experience of tolerating and managing fear and anxiety.

Dealing With Fear of Physical Sensations

Because this particular phobia involves fainting, which is managed by applied tension, and because there is pain associated with exposures to needles and injections, it is generally recommended that deliberate exposure to feared physical sensations *not* be included in the treatment for phobias of blood, needles, and injections.

Issues Unique to Blood, Injection, and Medical Phobias

Finding the Materials Needed for Treatment

For individuals with blood phobias, there are many good films depicting blood and surgery. These include popular films as well as films for medical education available from medical school libraries. Butcher shops and medical settings (e.g., hospital blood banks) are good sources for real blood. For people with needle phobias, begin with photos or films showing injections (see chapter 8 of the workbook for suggestions). In addition, devices used for finger-prick blood tests may be used. Finally, therapists who are not physicians should work in conjunction with a doctor, nurse, or laboratory technician who can administer blood tests or injections during the later stages of the exposure therapy. Similarly, therapists treating dental phobias should work with a dentist who can help expose clients to feared dental procedures.

Fainting

Blood and injection phobias are the only phobias often associated with a drop in blood pressure that may lead to fainting. In addition to the embarrassment of having this reaction, clients may have realistic concerns about hurting themselves when falling, or vomiting when unconscious. Precautions should be taken to protect the client during exposure practices. In the early stages of exposure therapy, when fainting is more likely, practices should be conducted in the presence of a helper. In addition, clients should consult a physician before conducting practices that may lead to fainting. Some medical conditions (e.g., cardiovascular disease) may increase the risks associated with fainting.

Difficulty Finding Veins

A proportion of individuals with needle phobias have veins that are small or difficult to find. People with small veins are more likely to experience pain and bruising during blood tests because their veins are hard to find.

This physical feature may make it more difficult for them to overcome the fear. Nevertheless, such individuals can still benefit from exposure (many individuals with small veins still receive blood tests without significant fear or avoidance, despite the pain). In addition, when they require blood work, they are to be encouraged to discuss their previous history of painful experiences with the technician and request that the most skilled technician at the clinic perform the procedure.

Applied Tension

Because blood and injection phobias are often associated with fainting, applied tension (tensing muscles to raise one's blood pressure and avoid fainting in the feared situation) is an effective treatment for individuals with these phobias (Öst, Fellenius, & Sterner, 1991).

As stated before, given the possibility of fainting and pain during exposures to needles, etc., we generally recommend *not* conducting deliberate induction to feared physical sensations in this type of phobia.

Case Examples

Alexis

Alexis was a 40-year-old teacher who was delaying surgery for removal of a benign tumor in her breast because she feared receiving a blood test before the surgery. Throughout her life, blood tests had been difficult because technicians had a hard time finding an appropriate vein into which to insert the needle. Because Alexis had small veins, it often took several tries to find a good vein, and Alexis usually ended up with mild bruising from the attempts. In fact, she typically had to have the blood taken from her hand or some location other than her arm. Her fear became a problem after a particularly painful experience with a blood test she had to get before college. The technician was relatively young and appeared to be somewhat inexperienced. Alexis warned her that it might be difficult to find a good vein in her arm and suggested that she try her hand. The technician tried the arm anyway and ended up engaging in what Alexis described as a "fishing expedition" in her arm, as she tried to "hook" a vein with the needle. Eventually, she ended up taking the blood from her hand and Alexis experienced significant pain and bruising that lasted for several days.

Alexis had good reason to fear blood tests. Her experience had taught her that blood tests were painful. Nevertheless, her reaction appeared to be out of proportion to the realistic danger. Most of her blood tests, although unpleasant, were not as difficult as the one she received before college. Alexis admitted that although it was natural for her to be apprehensive about blood tests, her reaction was excessive. She agreed to attempt an exposure-based treatment program. However, the treatment was modified in several ways. First, Alexis practiced requesting that she have a skilled and experienced technician take her blood. Second, given that technicians were never able to find a vein in her arm, she was instructed to insist that they not even try to do so but rather that they find the vein elsewhere. Methods of assertively insisting on these two conditions were practiced in the session, after which Alexis practiced these strategies during actual blood tests. Alexis responded very well to exposure therapy and was able to undergo her surgery. Although she continued to feel nervous before receiving blood tests, she reported that her anxiety was manageable and that she would no longer avoid blood work. ▪

Carlos

▪ *Carlos was a 25-year-old man who worked as bank teller and had been fearful of seeing blood ever since he first fainted in a high school health class. Since that time, he had avoided seeing or even talking about blood and medical procedures. Given Carlos's history of fainting, we recommended that Carlos ask his family physician if there was any medical reason (e.g., heart disease) why he should avoid situations that might trigger a vasovagal reaction. Carlos was in fine health, and his doctor was not concerned about his undergoing exposure therapy. Treatment began in the first session by teaching Carlos to use applied tension during exposure to videotaped surgery. Although he felt somewhat lightheaded, the applied tension successfully prevented fainting. Carlos was instructed to continue exposure at home while practicing applied tension over the next week. At the second session, exposure was continued, this time without the benefits of applied tension. During the first practice, Carlos felt as though he might faint. However, with repeated exposure to the films, his discomfort decreased. Toward the end of the session, the therapist used a lancet to prick his own finger while Carlos watched. Carlos reported only mild levels of anxiety. Treatment was terminated, and Carlos was instructed to continue practicing exposure on his own in the coming weeks.* ▓

Chapter 11   *Overcoming Claustrophobia*

(Corresponds to chapter 9 of the workbook)

Outline

- Discuss the nature of claustrophobia
- Instruct the client to identify phobic triggers and anxious thoughts and behaviors
- Discuss ways to locate situations for practicing exposure exercises
- Instruct the client to challenge anxious thoughts
- Remind the client of strategies for exposure exercises

Nature of Claustrophobia

This chapter in the workbook begins with an introduction to the nature of claustrophobia, including a definition of the disorder, a case example, and information on the epidemiology and etiology of this phobia.

Identifying Phobic Triggers and Anxious Thoughts and Behaviors

The initial step in the treatment of claustrophobia is to make a detailed functional analysis of the client's phobia. Specifically, clients are instructed to identify specific phobic cues in addition to listing the variables that influence the intensity of their fear when confronting the phobic stimulus. In addition, clients are taught to identify their anxious thoughts and the ways in which they avoid situations involving closed-in places. Ex-

haustive lists of typical phobic cues, thoughts, and behaviors are provided
to help clients identify these variables for their own phobias.

Locating Situations for Exposure Exercises

The "Finding Items Needed for Exposure" section in the workbook helps
clients locate the settings required for exposure practices. This section
includes suggestions for creating closed-in situations at home and for
finding claustrophobic situations outside the home.

Challenging Anxious Thoughts

Clients are instructed to change anxious thoughts by seeking out corrective
information and by identifying and challenging probability overestimations
and catastrophic thinking patterns. For probability overestimations, clients
are expected to look at all the evidence and consider the realistic odds for
whatever it is they are most worried about in relation to the phobic stimulus and, where appropriate, in relation to the physical sensations they experience in the context of the phobic stimulus. For catastrophizing,
clients are expected to face the worst and realize that it is not as bad as
first thought and to focus on ways of coping. Decatastrophizing is particularly suitable for worries about not being able to tolerate fear or the
physical sensations associated with fear.

Exposure-Based Strategies

Remind your client of specific strategies for conducting exposure practices, such as ensuring that sessions are constructed in way that will permit him or her to learn that whatever he or she is most worried about
rarely or never happens or that he or she can cope with the phobic stimulus and the accompanying anxiety. In addition, practices should be frequent, planned in advance, and challenging. For exposure to be beneficial, clients will most likely need to experience discomfort during the
exposure, especially since a critical learning experience is that of tolerating and managing fear and anxiety.

Dealing With Fear of Physical Sensations

Clients are encouraged to deal with their fear of sensations in the claustrophobic context by applying cognitive skills to their misappraisals of the bodily sensations and also by eventually deliberately inducing the feared physical sensations in claustrophobic situations. For example, they may deliberately over-breathe, wear heavy clothing, or practice very slow breathing to create the sensation of shortness of breath.

Issues Unique to Claustrophobia

Finding the Situations Needed for Treatment

Seek out a variety of enclosed places that might be appropriate for exposure practices. These may include elevators (especially older elevators, which tend to be smaller and slower than newer elevators), closets, small windowless rooms, desks (large enough for a client to sit under), basements, attics, caves, small cars, and other places listed in chapter 9 of the workbook.

Overlap With Panic Disorder

Of all the specific phobias, claustrophobia shares the most features with panic disorder (e.g., recurrent panic attacks characterized by an intense fear of certain physical sensations, such as breathlessness). In fact, many individuals with panic disorder report a fear of enclosed places as part of their pattern of phobic avoidance. Because of the similarities between panic disorder and claustrophobia, it is very important that therapists screen carefully for unexpected panic attacks (outside claustrophobic situations) and pervasive worry about panic attacks. Many clients with fears of enclosed places suffer from panic disorder with agoraphobia, rather than a specific phobia, in which case we recommend our *Mastery of Your Anxiety and Panic, Fourth Edition* (Barlow & Craske, 2006).

Shortness of Breath and Fear of Suffocation

Shortness of breath and a fear of suffocation are very prominent features of claustrophobia. Therefore, it may be especially helpful for clients with claustrophobia to use some of the strategies that have been shown to be useful for people with similar fears (e.g., individuals with panic disorder), including interoceptive exposure and cognitive restructuring.

Actually Getting Stuck in an Elevator

Although it rarely occurs, people occasionally do get stuck in elevators. Clients should prepare for this by considering how they would cope with actually getting stuck in an elevator. For example, the therapist might ask the client about the outcome for individuals who do get stuck in elevators. Most clients will report that, other than the inconvenience of being stuck, harm rarely comes to anyone whose elevator became stuck.

Fear of Fire or Earthquakes While in a Closed-in Situation

Fears of earthquakes or fire are common among individuals with claustrophobia. Facilitating exposure to the phobic situation and helping the client examine the realistic probability of fire and earthquakes occurring while he or she is in a closed-in place are usually effective.

Case Example

Jeffrey

Jeffrey was a 35-year-old business executive whose office recently moved to the 37th floor of a new office tower. Although he had been afraid of elevators and other enclosed places since his early teens, only now had his fear become a problem because of his having to be in an elevator for a prolonged period every day. Jeffrey's fear was complicated by his asthma; one of his biggest fears was that the shortness of breath he experienced in closed-in places might trigger an asthma attack.

The first step in Jeffrey's treatment was to determine the actual risk of his exposure leading to an asthma attack. During an interview, Jeffrey reported that his asthma is a problem only when he is exposed to cats or when he has a bad cold. He reported that other activities, including exercise, tended not to trigger his asthma. His physician confirmed that the symptoms Jeffrey experienced during exposure to enclosed places were unlikely to trigger an asthmatic reaction. In fact, Jeffrey was able to differentiate between the shortness of breath that he experienced when asthmatic (associated with wheezing) and the breathlessness that he felt in a closed-in place (associated with hyperventilation).

A standard exposure program was then developed and implemented. Jeffrey practiced standing in a closet with the door shut a number of times. Next, the lock on the door was reversed, so that it could not be opened from the inside. Jeffrey sat in the closet for a predetermined time (15 minutes), after which he was let out. His fear was quite high at first but, with repetition, gradually decreased to a mild level. He also practiced being in a locked stairwell.

By the third session, Jeffrey was ready to begin working on his fear of elevators. After practicing in other closed-in places, Jeffrey found that his fear of elevators had decreased significantly, although it was still quite high. Jeffrey was instructed to practice riding the elevator starting with 1 floor, and then 2 floors, and then progressing to 30 floors. Next, he entered an elevator at work after hours (when it was no longer being used by others) and avoided pushing any buttons, so that the elevator remained stationary (as if it were stuck). At first, Jeffrey could feel his heart racing, but, with repetition, his anxiety quickly decreased. He continued to practice riding elevators over the next week.

In the fourth session, Jeffrey combined interoceptive exposure exercises with his practices in elevators. Specifically, he practiced taking fast and very deep breaths to induce a breathless feeling while standing in an elevator (when no one else was around). This exercise induced mild feelings of anxiety, which quickly dissipated. By the end of the fourth session, Jeffrey was no longer afraid of elevators or the other closed-in situations that he frequently encountered. During a follow-up appointment one month later, Jeffrey reported having made further gains. ▪

Chapter 12   *Overcoming Animal and Insect Phobias*

(Corresponds to chapter 10 of the workbook)

Outline

- Discuss the nature of animal and insect phobias

- Instruct the client to identify phobic triggers and anxious thoughts and behaviors

- Discuss ways to find the items needed to practice exposure exercises

- Instruct the client to challenge anxious thoughts

- Remind the client of strategies for exposure exercises

Nature of Animal and Insect Phobias

This chapter in the workbook begins with an introduction to the nature of animal and insect phobias, including a definition of the disorder, case examples, and information on the epidemiology and etiology of these phobias.

Identifying Phobic Triggers and Anxious Thoughts and Behaviors

The initial step in the treatment of animal and insect phobias is to make a detailed functional analysis of the client's phobia. Specifically, clients are instructed to identify specific phobic cues and to list the variables that influence the intensity of their fear when confronting the phobic stimulus. In addition, clients are taught to identify their anxious thoughts and the ways in which they avoid encountering the animal they fear. Exhaustive lists of typical phobic cues, thoughts, and behaviors are provided to help clients identify these variables for their own phobias.

Finding Items Needed for Exposure Exercises

The "Finding Items Needed for Exposure" section in the workbook helps clients locate the objects and situations required for exposure practices. This section includes suggestions for obtaining photographs and videos showing the feared animal and for arranging to encounter the animal in real life.

Challenging Anxious Thoughts

Clients are instructed to change anxious thoughts by seeking out corrective information and by identifying and challenging probability overestimations and catastrophic thinking patterns. For probability overestimations, clients are expected to look at all the evidence and consider the realistic odds for whatever it is they are most worried about in relation to the phobic stimulus and, where appropriate, in relation to the physical sensations they experience in the context of the phobic stimulus. For catastrophizing, clients are expected to face the worst and realize that it is not as bad as first thought and to focus on ways of coping. Decatastrophizing is particularly suitable for worries about not being able to tolerate fear or other emotions such as disgust.

Exposure-Based Strategies

Remind your client of specific strategies for conducting exposure practices, such as ensuring that sessions are constructed to permit the client to learn that whatever he or she is most worried about rarely or never happens or that he or she can cope with the phobic stimulus and with the anxiety. In addition, practices should be frequent, planned in advance, and challenging. Clients should be informed that for exposure to be beneficial, they will most likely need to experience discomfort during the practice sessions, especially since a critical learning experience is the experience of tolerating and managing fear and anxiety.

Dealing With Fear of Physical Sensations

In most cases, individuals who are phobic of animals show little fear of the physical sensations of anxiety when encountering their phobic stimulus. However, in the event that your client does report fears of physical sensations (e.g., I am afraid that when I approach the spider, my heart will beat so fast that I will have a heart attack), encourage them to engage in cognitive restructuring regarding the meaning of the symptoms and to eventually incorporate deliberate induction of physical sensations in the phobic context, such as by consuming caffeine or running up a flight of stairs before approaching the spider.

Issues Unique to Animal and Insect Phobias

Finding Materials Needed for Treatment

The specific materials needed will depend on the type of animal. For individuals with spider or insect phobias, the phobic stimuli can often be found in basements, fields, gardens, and so on. The easiest time to find spiders outside is early in the morning when there is still dew on the spider webs, making them more visible. Moths are easiest to find at night, flying around porch lights. Bees are of course often found near flowers. There are a variety of other places where insects and spiders may be found. Entomologists in university biology departments, science museums, and in zoos may supply specific insects. Exterminators may have access to a variety of creatures as well. Beekeepers are likely to have a supply of bees on hand (including those that do not sting). Finally, certain insects and spiders may be ordered through the mail. Several companies sell spiders and insects to biological researchers (for example, the Carolina Biological Supply Company, http://www.carolina.com). In addition, ant-farm companies will mail you ants for a relatively small fee.

Good sources for larger animals (e.g., mice, dogs, cats, birds, snakes) include pet stores, friends, co-workers and relatives who own these pets, breeders, the Humane Society, and the zoo. In addition, clients may have neighbors or friends who can supply these animals.

Find ways to restrain the animal during exposure practices. For insects and spiders, it is helpful to have clear jars and tubs for the insect to move around in the client's view. For snakes, an aquarium is useful. For dogs and cats, small cages, leashes, and harnesses can be used to restrain the animal.

When working with birds, it is important to have access to a cage. In addition, where possible, use birds with clipped wings. It is important to learn how to properly care for the animals you are using for exposure practices.

The workbook includes ideas for where to get relevant books, videos, and other stimuli. Generally, books and videos depicting animals are available at large bookstores and nature stores. Realistic replicas of snakes, insects, lizards, and other animals can often be found in toy stores, museum stores, and nature stores.

Unpredictability of the Animal

Unlike other feared objects and situations, animals and insects are inherently unpredictable. We cannot control when or how they move during an exposure session. This is particularly the case for animals that can fly (e.g., birds, some insects). Throughout treatment, make every effort to control the animal's behavior. Knowing something about the specific animal often helps. For example, snakes are sometimes less friendly when they are shedding or it is near their feeding time. Also, some animals may not like to be restrained. Speaking to the pet owner (if the animal is borrowed) about the nature of the treatment might help you anticipate and prevent difficulties. Of course, one cannot predict or control every aspect of an animal's behavior. For example, we once had a snake "relieve itself" on a client. Fortunately, it was near the end of treatment and the client had a good sense of humor.

Protecting the Client

Unfortunately, fears of animals and insects are not completely irrational. Sometimes animals can be dangerous. Bees can sting, dogs can bite, and cats can scratch. The therapist is responsible for the client's safety, so he or she should be familiar with the animal being used and should know something about its behavior (e.g., its tendency to bite). The therapist should not ask the client to do anything that is dangerous (e.g., touch a bee, approach a stray dog that is growling). We suggest that before using any spider for exposure it be identified in a field guide to determine whether its bite is dangerous.

Killing Animals/Insects Versus Removing Them From the Home

Although clients often prefer to kill feared insects and spiders when they see them, we typically recommend that they catch the animal or insect and remove it from the home. A decision not to kill the animal is more consistent with the message that the animal is not dangerous.

Case Example

Sara

Sara was a 14-year-old high school student who had had an intense fear of spiders for as long as she could remember. Her fear intensified when she moved to a lakeside house where there were many spiders. In fact, she saw spiders almost daily. Sara's family was aware of her fear and took it upon themselves to protect Sara from seeing spiders whenever possible. To protect herself from spiders, Sara never wore shorts. When she went to sleep, she always slept in her clothes, used a heavy blanket, and kept the windows closed. In the summer, her room was so hot that she wrapped ice cubes in a towel and used it to cool herself off rather than opening her window or sleeping with a lighter sheet.

At the beginning of treatment, Sara refused to be anywhere near a spider. In fact, just talking about spiders during the evaluation made her very anxious. Treatment began by having her practice saying the word "spider." After saying the word "spider" for a few minutes, we increased the intensity of the exposure by saying the phrase "big hairy spider." By the end of the first session, Sara was able to touch pictures of a spider in a photo book. Sarah was instructed to practice touching these photos at home in the week between her first and second treatment sessions.

When Sara came for the second session, she had not completed her homework, although she was still able to touch the spider photos in the therapist's office with only moderate discomfort. When asked why she had not done her homework, Sara explained that her week had been too busy and she had been unable to find the time to complete the assignment. Further enquiry revealed that Sara had avoided the homework because of her anxiety. During this session, we began exposure to a live spider. Sara was at one end of a large room with the therapist holding a spider in a jar at the other end. Gradually, Sara practiced approaching the spider, so that by the end of the hour she was able to hold the jar comfortably. Sara was sent home with the jar and instructed to practice holding the jar for 30 minutes a day until the next session.

After two days, Sara phoned to say that the jar was in her garage and that she was too afraid to bring the jar into her house. We agreed that we would discuss the issue at our next session, and her homework assignment was suspended for the rest of the week. Sara was asked to attend the next session with a parent who might be able to help her with her practices at home. Sara's father joined her for the next two sessions.

During the third session, Sara reported that her fear was much higher at home than in the therapist's office. After some discussion, it appeared that two variables might be responsible for the difference. First, the presence of a therapist seemed to make exposure practices easier. Second, having the spider in her own home was more difficult than seeing it elsewhere. Sara's father was given the rationale for treatment and was instructed to read relevant parts of the workbook so he could help Sara complete her exposure homework assignments. For the second part of the session, Sara practiced being near a spider that had been released in a large plastic tub. She was *instructed to repeat this exercise at home with the supervision and help of her father.*

During the fourth session, Sara's anxiety was significantly lower. Within 15 minutes, she was able to touch the spider with her finger, and by the end of the session she experienced only mild fear as the spider crawled on her. Again she was instructed to repeat this exposure at home and to have her father gradually withdraw from the process (e.g., leave the room while Sara was handling a spider). After five days, Sara phoned to say that she was completely over her fear. She had stopped her overprotective behaviors (e.g., sleeping with the windows closed) and no longer needed her family to protect her from seeing spiders. We discussed some strategies for maintaining her gains, and no further sessions were scheduled. ▪

Chapter 13 | *Overcoming Height Phobias*

(Corresponds to chapter 11 of the workbook)

Outline

- Discuss the nature of height phobias

- Instruct the client to identify phobic triggers and anxious thoughts and behaviors

- Discuss ways to locate situations for practicing exposure exercises

- Instruct the client to challenge anxious thoughts

- Remind the client of strategies for exposure exercises

Nature of Height Phobias

Chapter 11 in the workbook begins with an introduction to the nature of height phobias, including a definition of the disorder, a case example, and information on the epidemiology and etiology of this phobia.

Identifying Phobic Triggers and Anxious Thoughts and Behaviors

The initial step in the treatment of height phobias is to make a detailed functional analysis of the client's phobia. Specifically, clients are instructed to identify specific phobic cues and list the variables that influence the intensity of their fear when confronting feared high places. In addition, clients are taught to identify their anxious thoughts and the ways in which they avoid situations involving heights. Exhaustive lists of typical phobic cues, thoughts, and behaviors are provided to help clients identify these variables for their own phobias.

Locating Situations for Exposure Exercises

The section "Finding the Situations Needed for Exposure" helps clients locate the settings and situations required for exposure practices.

Challenging Anxious Thoughts

Clients are instructed to change anxious thoughts by seeking out corrective information and by identifying and challenging probability overestimations and catastrophic thinking patterns. For probability overestimations, clients are expected to look at all the evidence and consider the realistic odds for whatever it is they are most worried about in relation to the phobic stimulus and, where appropriate, in relation to the physical sensations they experience in the context of the phobic stimulus. For catastrophizing, clients are expected to face the worst and realize that it is not as bad as first thought and to focus on ways of coping. Decatastrophizing is particularly suitable for worries about not being able to tolerate fear or the physical sensations associated with fear.

Exposure-Based Strategies

Remind your client of specific strategies for conducting exposure practices, such as ensuring that sessions are constructed to permit the client to learn that whatever he or she is most worried about rarely or never happens or that he or she can cope with the phobic stimulus and accompanying anxiety. In addition, practices should be frequent, planned in advance, and challenging. For exposure to be beneficial, clients will most likely need to experience discomfort during the exposure, especially since a critical learning experience is the experience of tolerating and managing fear and anxiety.

Dealing With Fear of Physical Sensations

Clients are encouraged to deal with their fear of sensations in the height context by applying the cognitive skills to their misappraisals of the bodily sensations and also by eventually deliberately inducing the feared physical sensations in high situations. For example, they may deliberately tense their body to create a sensation of shakiness or weakness when they are facing heights.

Issues Unique to Height Phobias

Finding the Situations Needed for Treatment

Clients should be encouraged to seek out a variety of high places that might be appropriate for exposure practices. These may include tall buildings, amusement park rides, bridges, fire escapes, stadiums, and other situations listed in chapter 11 of the workbook.

The Role of Physical Sensations

Many individuals with height phobias report feeling anxious over the sensations they feel in the phobic situation. These sensations may include a sense of imbalance, "rubbery" legs, and dizziness. Assuming that these problems are not medically based (e.g., an individual with inner-ear difficulties would have balance problems across a range of situations, not just when up high), encourage clients to continue practicing despite the sensations. If there is reason to believe that a client has difficulty with coordination or balance, as may be the case in some elderly individuals, be cautious in designing exposure practices and do not deliberately induce feared physical sensations.

Coping With the Urge to Jump From a High Place

Individuals who have an intense urge to jump when in a high place should be reassured that the urges are normal for people with height phobias and that they are extremely unlikely to act on these urges (assuming they are not acutely suicidal). Such urges are an example of the fear of doing something uncontrolled that often accompanies panic attacks.

Concern About Being Pushed Over the Edge by Another Person

This fear is common among individuals with height phobias. It is best dealt with by having the client practice standing in a high place while other people walk behind him or her. With repeated exposure, the fear usually decreases. In addition, cognitive strategies may be useful for decreasing this fear (e.g., asking the client what the realistic odds are of being pushed by another person).

Case Example

Ella

■ *Ella was a 67-year-old woman who had recently retired and was looking forward to traveling across the country with her husband the next summer. However, she had a long history of height phobia and was apprehensive about having to travel over bridges and other high places on her trip. For example, she was unable to spend time on her fourth-floor balcony or to sit in high seats at the theater. She had attempted a variety of treatments in the past, including anxiolytic medication, hypnosis, and two sessions of behavior therapy, which involved exposure to high bridges. After noticing no change in her fear after two sessions, she discontinued her behavioral treatment. Her primary concern was that she might purposely drive her car off the bridge or might lose control and jump from a high place.*

Treatment began with an overview of cognitive restructuring. Ella was given the rationale for treatment and was taught to recognize her thoughts about driving or jumping off a high place as overestimations. She was reassured that although this worry is very common among people who fear heights, she was extremely unlikely to jump or to drive her car off a bridge. She agreed to attempt exposure again, this time combining it with appropriate cognitive strategies and making a commitment to stick with the exposure for a longer period.

During the first exposure session, Ella practiced standing in the top row of a theater and looking down. Because of sustained exposure with high fear levels, Ella was eventually able to recognize that it was very unlikely that she would jump from the ledge. She was instructed to practice visiting the same spot with her husband several times over the next week.

Ella had three more treatment sessions in similar situations. In the fifth session, she began practicing driving over bridges. Ella drove across the bridge repeatedly in the 90-minute session, and she continued to practice crossing the bridge over the coming week.

Although Ella's fear did not decrease as quickly as that of many clients, her fear did decrease significantly after about 10 sessions and many practices between sessions. She still had some anxiety about her upcoming trip, but she was determined to overcome the fear and planned to practice repeated exposure to difficult situations that might arise while traveling. She reported no longer having significant fear when encountering heights during her normal routine. ▪

Chapter 14 *Overcoming Driving Phobias*

(Corresponds to chapter 12 of the workbook)

Outline

- Discuss the nature of driving phobias

- Teach the client to realistically evaluate his or her driving skills

- Instruct the client to identify phobic triggers and anxious thoughts and behaviors

- Discuss ways to locate situations for practicing exposure exercises

- Instruct the client to challenge anxious thoughts

- Remind the client of strategies for exposure exercises

Nature of Driving Phobias

Chapter 12 in the workbook begins with an introduction to the nature of driving phobias, including a definition of the disorder, a case example, and information on the epidemiology and etiology of this phobia.

Evaluation of Driving Skills

Clients are to conduct a realistic evaluation of their driving skills; many individuals who fear driving avoid being behind the wheel and may lack the experience and knowledge to be a safe and effective driver. Clients who have weak driving skills are encouraged to consider taking driving lessons.

Identifying Phobic Triggers and Anxious Thoughts and Behaviors

The initial step in treating driving phobias is to conduct a detailed functional analysis of the client's phobia. Clients are instructed to identify specific phobic cues in addition to listing the variables that influence the intensity of their fear when confronting the phobic stimulus. Clients are taught to identify their anxious thoughts and the ways in which they avoid situations involving driving. Exhaustive lists of typical phobic cues, thoughts, and behaviors are provided to help clients identify these variables for their own phobias.

Locating Situations for Exposure Exercises

The "Finding Items Needed for Exposure" section in the workbook helps clients locate the settings and vehicles required for exposure practices.

Challenging Anxious Thoughts

Clients are instructed to change anxious thoughts by seeking out corrective information and by identifying and challenging probability overestimations and catastrophic thinking patterns. For probability overestimations, clients are expected to look at all the evidence and consider the realistic odds for whatever it is they are most worried about in relation to the phobic stimulus and, where appropriate, in relation to the physical sensations they experience in the context of the phobic stimulus. For catastrophizing, clients are expected to face the worst and realize that it is not as bad as first thought and to focus on ways of coping. Decatastrophizing is particularly suitable for worries about not being able to tolerate fear or the physical sensations that are often associated with fear.

Exposure-Based Strategies

Remind your client of specific strategies for conducting exposure practices, such as ensuring that sessions are constructed to permit the client to learn that whatever he or she is most worried about rarely or never happens or that he or she can cope with the phobic stimulus and with the anxiety. In addition, practices should be frequent, planned in advance, and challenging. For exposure to be beneficial, clients will most likely need to experience discomfort during the exposure, especially since a critical learning experience is learning to tolerate and manage fear and anxiety.

Dealing With Fear of Physical Sensations

Clients are encouraged to manage their fear of sensations in driving situations by applying the cognitive skills to their misappraisals of the bodily sensations and also by eventually deliberately inducing the feared physical sensations in driving situations. For example, they may deliberately turn on the heater to feel hot, or deliberately tense their arms to feel shaky when they drive.

Issues Unique to Driving Phobias

Finding the Situations Needed for Treatment

Individuals who fear driving need access to a car and a valid driver's license. Clients who fear being a passenger may need to work with a friend or family member who is able to drive them around. If the therapist is willing to drive clients around, the client should first sign a waiver of responsibility. To be safe, we also recommend that the therapist check with his or her lawyer and/or insurance company to ensure adequate protection in case of an accident (a waiver may not always be enough). Generally, we recommend that clients do not drive the therapist's car.

The Role of Physical Impairments

Some individuals with driving phobias will report having difficulties hearing or seeing (e.g., poor night vision) that impair their ability to drive. Such individuals should consult their doctor to assess whether they do in fact have impairments that might interfere with driving safely. Similarly, some individuals may have motor impairments limiting their ability to react quickly in certain situations. Assess the nature of these impairments and acknowledge these limitations if appropriate. Clients should not be asked to do anything that is in fact dangerous.

Fear of Physical Sensations

Individuals with driving phobias often fear the sensations they feel when they are anxious (e.g., dizziness, breathlessness). Instruct clients not to fight these feelings but rather to continue practicing despite the sensations. Later in treatment, the sensations can be deliberately induced, such as by tensing muscles while driving, so that the client can eventually becoming less afraid of the sensations.

In cases where it is suspected that intense physical sensations might actually impair the client's ability to drive safely (e.g., the degree of shakiness in the legs interferes with the use of the brake and accelerator pedals), clients can begin by practice driving slowly on quiet streets or in large parking lots on the weekends. However, in most cases, driving is unlikely not to be significantly impaired by these sensations.

Case Example

Joanne

Joanne was a 36-year-old woman who worked part-time as a cashier. She reported a fear of driving ever since she began learning to drive at age 16. During a particular driving lesson with her older sister, Joanne was waiting to turn left at an intersection when the light turned red. As she sat in the middle of the intersection, her sister became angry, and other drivers honked their horns to signal her to get out of the way. Joanne froze and asked her sister to take the wheel. After that episode, she never drove again. Her primary fears were related to making a mistake leading to embarrassment or a car accident. She finally presented for treatment when she was transferred to a store that was not easily accessible by public transportation.

Joanne did not have a driver's license, so the first step was to have her get a learner's permit. Next she was given the rationale for treatment. In the second session, she was introduced to cognitive restructuring, and Joanne practiced challenging her beliefs regarding other drivers' evaluations of her skills. During session three, Joanne was given the rationale for exposure therapy and was instructed to practice driving short distances with her husband.

She returned the next week, having tried twice to practice driving, only to stop each time following arguments with her husband about her driving skills. According to Joanne's report, her husband repeatedly became frustrated and angry with her minor driving mistakes. Because Joanne had only a learner's permit and required a licensed driver to be with her in the car, her husband's participation was important. Joanne brought her husband with her to the next session. A behavioral test was administered during which Joanne drove with her husband in the passenger seat and the therapist in the back seat. Her husband was quite critical of her driving, which appeared to increase her anxiety. Despite her husband's criticisms, Joanne exhibited good driving skills, especially in light of her limited driving experience.

Joanne's husband acknowledged that his comments were not helpful, and he agreed to participate in the remaining treatment sessions to learn how he could be more constructive. The treatment rationale was reviewed, with a special emphasis on instructing Joanne's husband to be more supportive when they were driving together. In addition, Joanne decided to take driving lessons to improve her driving skills.

Over the next four sessions, Joanne's husband more or less stopped his critical comments, and Joanne was experiencing less anxiety when driving. Joanne began her driving classes and was practicing regularly between treatment sessions. Because left turns were still particularly difficult for Joanne, we began to practice turning left over and over again. The next two sessions were spent practicing becoming embarrassed when driving.

Joanne was told to purposely make very minor "mistakes" as she drove, without doing anything dangerous. For example, she was instructed to drive a bit too slowly and to wait briefly when the light turned green. With practice, she became used to the comments and honking of other drivers and was less concerned about becoming embarrassed when she made a mistake.

Joanne's anxiety over driving (and her driving skills) improved markedly by the twelfth session. In addition, she obtained her driver's license and planned to buy her own car soon. ▪

Chapter 15   *Overcoming Flying Phobias*

(Corresponds to chapter 13 of the workbook)

Outline

- Discuss the nature of flying phobias

- Instruct the client to identify phobic triggers and anxious thoughts and behaviors

- Discuss ways to locate situations for practicing exposure exercises

- Instruct the client to challenge anxious thoughts

- Remind the client of strategies for exposure exercises

Nature of Flying Phobias

Chapter 13 in the workbook begins with an introduction to the nature of flying phobias, including a definition of the disorder, a case example, and information on the epidemiology and etiology of this phobia.

Identifying Phobic Triggers and Anxious Thoughts and Behaviors

The initial step in the treatment of flying phobia is to make a detailed functional analysis of the client's fear. Clients are instructed to identify specific phobic cues and the variables that influence the intensity of their fear when confronting the phobic situation. In addition, clients are taught to identify their anxious thoughts and the ways in which they avoid situations involving flying. Exhaustive lists of typical phobic cues, thoughts, and behaviors are provided to help clients identify these variables for their own phobias.

Locating Situations for Exposure

The "Finding Items Needed for Exposure" section in the workbook helps clients locate the settings required for exposure practices. These include suggestions for imaginal exposure and real-life exposure practices. New virtual-reality treatments for fear of flying are also discussed, as are airline programs that specialize in helping people overcome flying phobias.

Challenging Anxious Thoughts

Clients are instructed to change anxious thoughts by seeking out corrective information and by identifying and challenging probability overestimations and catastrophic thinking patterns. For probability overestimations, clients are expected to look at all the evidence and consider the realistic odds for whatever it is they are most worried about in relation to the phobic stimulus and, where appropriate, in relation to the physical sensations they experience in the context of the phobic stimulus. For catastrophizing, clients are expected to face the worst and realize that it is not as bad as first thought and to focus on ways of coping (assuming that the client's prediction is *not* that the plane will crash!). Decatastrophizing is particularly suitable for worries about not being able to tolerate fear or the physical symptoms that often occur in the context of fear.

Exposure-Based Strategies

Remind your client of specific strategies for conducting exposure practices, such as ensuring that sessions are constructed to permit the client to learn that whatever he or she is most worried about rarely or never happens or that he or she can cope with the phobic stimulus and accompanying anxiety. In addition, practices should be frequent, planned in advance, and challenging. For exposure to be beneficial, clients will most likely need to experience discomfort during the practice sessions, especially since a critical learning experience is learning to tolerate and manage fear and anxiety.

Dealing With Fear of Physical Sensations

Clients are encouraged to deal with their fear of sensations in flight by applying the cognitive skills to their misappraisals of the bodily sensations and also by eventually deliberately inducing the feared physical sensations in flights. For example, they might deliberately not turn on the air vent, or they might drink a cup of coffee.

Issues Unique to Flying Phobias

Finding the Situations Needed for Treatment

The main difficulty in treating flying phobias is that the expense of flying makes it difficult to engage in repeated exposure practices. Clients should be encouraged to fly on commercial flights as often as they can afford. In addition, they may be able to arrange to spend time on airplanes on the ground. Occasionally, private pilots can be hired to fly with clients in small planes. Often, just having some information about flying (e.g., statistics about the actual risks) can be helpful. For example, more than one billion people fly safely each year; only several hundred passengers are involved in accidents. In fact, the most dangerous part of any flight is the drive to the airport. Some statistics on the safety of flying are provided in the workbook, and many more are reported in various books listed in the Recommended Readings section at the end of this guide.

One Cannot Escape From an Airplane

Because it is virtually impossible to safely escape from an airborne airplane, exposure to flying can be very anxiety provoking, and many clients are reluctant to practice flying. Allowing clients to initially rely on safety signals (e.g., being accompanied, taking medication) helps make exposure more manageable. After several successful flights, clients should be encouraged to stop using safety signals.

Plane Crashes Are Often Fatal

Clients will often use this argument to support their belief that flying is dangerous. In such cases, inform clients of the statistics showing that the chances of a particular airplane crashing are virtually zero. It is important to help clients recognize their tendency to overestimate the likelihood of crashing.

Case Example

Michael

Michael was a 45-year-old businessman who feared flying. Although he rarely avoided flying, he used a variety of maladaptive coping strategies, including distraction (e.g., listening to music, reading), drinking four to five alcoholic drinks on the airplane, taking 20 mg or more of diazepam, and staying awake the entire night before the flight so that he would be tired on the airplane. His work required him to fly two or three times per year; however, because of his use of alcohol, medication, and sleep deprivation, his functioning on his business trips was often impaired. Michael was particularly nervous about flying on small airplanes.

During his evaluation, Michael reported that his primary fear while flying was that the plane might crash, although he also feared that he might lose control and embarrass himself if his anxiety became too high. Michael was seen for two treatment sessions before his first flight. During his first session, the rationale for treatment was presented. In addition, he was taught to identify specific beliefs regarding flying and was given methods of changing his anxious thoughts. Michael was instructed to read the book, Flying Without Fear (Brown, 1996; see the Recommended Reading at the end of this book) to learn more about the flight process and safety statistics. During the second session, Michael was given information on how to conduct exposure therapy. In particular, he was told to fly more frequently and to eliminate the overprotective behaviors and subtle forms of avoidance on which he relied. In addition, he was taught to accept his anxious feelings rather than fight them.

After his flight, Michael scheduled a third appointment. He reported that he was able to fly without relying on medication or sleep deprivation before the flight. Although he had two glasses of wine before his first flight, this was viewed as a success because it was much less alcohol than he had used during previous flights. During his flight home, he had only one glass of wine. Although Michael was still very anxious while flying, he noticed some improvement across each flight. He decided to schedule some additional short commuter flights weekly over the next month.

Michael's next appointment was a month later. He still was anxious before boarding airplanes but was better able to function without alcohol or the other strategies that he had previously used. He continued to fly, and he noticed that each flight was easier than the one before. In addition, he was better able to use cognitive strategies to manage his fear. ▪

Chapter 16 — *Overcoming Phobias of Storms, Water, Choking, and Vomiting*

(Corresponds to chapter 14 of the workbook)

Outline

- Discuss the nature of storm, water, choking, and vomiting phobias
- Instruct the client to identify phobic triggers and anxious thoughts and behaviors
- Provide instructions for imaginal exposure
- Instruct the client to challenge anxious thoughts
- Remind the client of strategies for exposure exercises

Nature of Storm, Water, Choking, and Vomiting Phobias

Chapter 14 of the workbook is divided into sections discussing fears of storms, choking and vomiting, and water. Each section begins with an introduction to the nature of the phobia, including a definition and information on epidemiology and etiology.

Identifying Phobic Triggers and Anxious Thoughts and Behaviors

The initial step in the treatment of any specific phobia is to make a detailed functional analysis of the client's phobia. Clients are instructed to identify specific phobic cues and the variables that influence the intensity of their fear when confronting the phobic stimulus. In addition, clients are taught to identify their anxious thoughts and the ways in which they avoid situations that they fear.

Imaginal Exposure

Instructions are provided for conducting imaginal exposure to situations that are difficult to create in real life (thunderstorms). Imaginal exposure is best used to complement real-life exposure.

Challenging Anxious Thoughts

Clients are instructed to change anxious thoughts by seeking out corrective information and by identifying and challenging probability overestimations and catastrophic thinking patterns. For probability overestimations, clients are expected to look at all the evidence and consider the realistic odds for whatever it is they are most worried about in relation to the phobic stimulus and, where appropriate, in relation to the physical sensations they experience in the context of the phobic stimulus. For catastrophizing, clients are expected to face the worst and realize that it is not as bad as first thought and to focus on ways of coping. Decatastrophizing is particularly suitable for worries about not being able to tolerate fear or the physical sensations associated with fear.

Exposure-Based Strategies

Remind your client of specific strategies for conducting exposure practices, such as ensuring that sessions are constructed to permit the client to learn that whatever he or she is most worried about rarely or never happens or that he or she can cope with the phobic stimulus and accompanying anxiety. In addition, practices should be frequent, planned in advance, and challenging. For exposure to be beneficial, clients will most likely need to experience discomfort during the exposure, especially since a critical learning experience is learning to tolerate and manage fear and anxiety.

Dealing With Fear of Physical Sensations

Clients are encouraged to deal with their fear of sensations by applying the cognitive skills to their misappraisals of the bodily sensations and also by eventually deliberately inducing the feared physical sensations in the phobic context.

Issues Specific to Each Type of Phobia

Individual sections discuss specific issues that arise when treating phobias of storms, choking, vomiting, and being in water.

Issues Unique to Storm Phobias

One cannot create storms for exposure practices. Unfortunately, storms cannot be created on demand for the purpose of exposure practices. Therefore, one must take advantage of storms when they do occur. One method of doing this is arranging an "on call" system, in which the therapist and client make contact when a storm occurs and discuss the steps to be taken. In addition, in case the therapist cannot contact the client, it can be helpful for the client to have detailed instructions regarding exposure practices to be conducted in case of a storm (e.g., look out the window, open the door). Finally, for some individuals, simulated exposure (using audiotapes of thunderstorms, films, imaginal exposure, or virtual-reality exposure) may be somewhat effective. Audiotaped recordings of thunderstorms are available at most large music stores and nature stores. Additional suggestions are provided in the workbook.

How far should exposure go? Exposure practices should not involve activities that are potentially dangerous. For example, clients should not be asked to stand under a tree in the middle of a field during a thunderstorm. On the other hand, it is probably perfectly safe to stand near a window during a thunderstorm.

Storms are infrequent. Because storms may be infrequent, clients may not have a sufficient number of practices, and fear may return between sessions. For this reason, storm phobias are more difficult to treat, relative to some other specific phobias. The suggestions listed earlier provide some ideas for "getting the most" out of each storm.

An Issue Unique to Water Phobias

The client may not be able to swim. It is not unrealistic to fear being in deep water if one cannot swim. However, it may be unrealistic to fear other water-related situations, including taking baths, being on a large boat, or being near water (e.g., on a beach or a dock). Exposure to these situations is likely to be safe, if proper precautions are taken (e.g., wearing a life jacket in a boat). Swimming lessons may be useful for individuals who cannot swim.

Issues Unique to Choking and Vomiting Phobias

Fear of physical sensations. Compared to some other specific phobias, phobias of choking and vomiting are more often associated with intense anxiety over specific physical sensations, particularly those that remind the client of a choking feeling or a feeling that he or she may vomit. These fears of sensations may occur regardless of location (at home, in public, etc). Feared sensations often include nausea, tightness in the throat, and other uncomfortable feelings. This fear of sensations is similar to that reported by clients with panic disorder and may respond to standard panic-management strategies, including cognitive restructuring and interoceptive exposure (See *Mastery of Your Anxiety and Panic, Fourth Edition* (Barlow & Craske, 2006). A variety of exercises may be used for inducing feared sensations. Spinning is often useful for inducing nausea. Wearing restrictive clothing (e.g., tie, scarf, turtleneck) or using a tongue depressor can induce a tightness in the throat or a gagging sensation.

Fear of eating particular foods. Individuals with choking and vomiting phobias often avoid eating foods they perceive as likely to cause choking, vomiting, or particular feared sensations. Clients should be encouraged to eat these foods, beginning with easier foods and moving up their hierarchy to more difficult foods.

Case Example

Cynthia

Cynthia was a 27-year-old woman who had had a fear of vomiting since childhood. Her fear had gradually worsened such that at the time she began treatment, she could eat only a handful of foods for fear that she might become nauseated and vomit. In addition, she avoided any activities that might lead to a tightness around her throat (e.g., wearing a turtleneck or a scarf), a gagging sensation (e.g., using a tongue depressor), or a feeling of having a "lump in her throat" (e.g., watching sad movies that might make her cry). She avoided being in situations where she might see vomit (e.g., her daughter's school, public bathrooms) and felt very uncomfortable even talking about the subject of vomiting. Cynthia did not recall the onset of her phobia, although she recalls vomiting as a young child without feeling frightened.

At the beginning of her treatment, a detailed exposure hierarchy was developed. Exposure practices began with her eating increasingly difficult foods during and between treatment sessions. Over the first six sessions, Cynthia became much less fearful of eating most of the foods on her hierarchy. At the same time, she practiced wearing scarves and tight collars until she was more comfortable with the sensation of tightness around her neck. After her sixth session, she began exposure to more difficult situations, including exposure to videos depicting vomiting, visiting her daughter's school, and inducing gagging with a tongue depressor. By the end of treatment, her fear had decreased significantly. She still reported that she would feel fearful if she were to vomit, but she no longer avoided situations that might trigger the feeling that she might vomit.

Recommended Reading

Specific Phobias and Related Topics

Antony, M. M., & Barlow, D. H. (2002). Specific phobia. In D. H. Barlow (Ed.), *Anxiety and its disorders: The nature and treatment of anxiety and panic* (2nd ed.) (pp. 380–417). New York: Guilford.

Antony, M. M., & McCabe, R. E. (2003). Anxiety disorders: Social and specific phobias. In A. Tasman, J. Kay, & J. A. Lieberman (Eds.), *Psychiatry*, 2nd ed. (pp. 1298–1330). Chichester, UK: Wiley.

Antony, M. M., & Swinson, R. P. (2000). *Phobic disorders and panic in adults: A guide to assessment and treatment.* Washington, DC: American Psychological Association.

Barlow, D. H. (2002). *Anxiety and its disorders: The nature and treatment of anxiety and panic, second edition.* New York: Guilford.

Bruce, T. J., & Sanderson, W. C. (1998). *Specific phobias: Clinical applications of evidence-based psychotherapy.* Northvale, NJ: Jason Aronson.

Craske, M. G. (1999). *Anxiety Disorders: Psychological approaches to theory and treatment.* Boulder, CO: Westview.

Craske, M. G. (2003). *Origins of phobias and anxiety disorders: Why more women than men?* Oxford, UK: Elsevier.

Craske, M. G., Hermans, D., & Vansteenwegen, D. (Eds.) (2006). *Fear and learning: From basic processes to clinical implications.* American Psychological Association.

Davey, G. C. L. (1997). *Phobias: A handbook of theory, research, and treatment.* Chichester, UK: Wiley.

Maj, M., Akiskal, H. S., López-Ibor, J. J., & Okasha, A. (2004). *Phobias.* New York: Wiley.

McCabe, R. E., & Antony, M. M. (2002). Specific and social phobias. In M. M. Antony & D. H. Barlow (Eds.), *Handbook of assessment and treatment planning psychological disorders* (pp. 113–146). New York: Guilford.

Rowa, K., McCabe, R. E., & Antony, M. M. (2006). Specific phobias. In F. Andrasik (Ed.), *Comprehensive handbook of personality and psycho-*

pathology, Volume 2: Adult psychopathology (pp. 154–168). Hoboken, NJ: John Wiley and Sons.

Animal Phobia

Antony, M. M., & McCabe, R. E. (2005). *Overcoming animal and insect phobias: How to conquer fear of dogs, snakes, rodents, bees, spiders, and more.* Oakland, CA: New Harbinger.

Blood and Needle Phobia

Antony, M. M., & Watling, M. (2006). *Overcoming medical phobias: How to conquer fear of blood, needles, doctors, and dentists.* Oakland, CA: New Harbinger.

Driving Phobia

Joseph, J. (2003). *110 car and driving emergencies and how to survive them: The complete guide to staying safe on the road.* Guilford, CT: Lyons.

Triffitt, J. (2003). *Back in the driver's seat: Understanding, challenging and managing the fear of driving.* Tasmania, Australia: Dr. Jacqui Triffitt. Copies of this book may be ordered from http://www.backinthedrivers seat.com.au.

Flying Phobia

Akers-Douglas, A., & Georgiou, G. (1996). *Flying? No fear! A handbook for apprehensive fliers.* West Sussex, UK: Summersdale.

Brown, D. (1996). *Flying without fear.* Oakland, CA: New Harbinger.

Cronin, J. (1998). *Your flight questions answered by a jetliner pilot.* Vergennes, VT: Plymouth.

Evans, J. (1997). *All you ever wanted to know about flying: The passenger's guide to how airliners fly.* Osceola, WI: Motorbooks International.

Hartman, C., & Huffaker, J. S. (1995). *The fearless flyer: How to fly in comfort and without trepidation.* Portland, OR: Eighth Mountain.

Seaman, D. (1998). *The fearless flier's handbook: Learning to beat the fear of flying with the experts from the Qantas Clinic.* Berkeley, CA: Ten Speed.

Smith, P. (2004). *Ask the pilot: Everything you need to know about air travel.* New York: Riverhead.

Height Phobia

Antony, M. M., & Rowa, K. (2007). *Overcoming fear of heights.* Oakland, CA: New Harbinger.

References

American Psychiatric Association. (2000). *Diagnostic and statistical manual of mental disorders (4th ed. Text revision)*. Washington, DC: American Psychiatric Association.

Antony, M. M. (2001). Measures for specific phobia. In M. M. Antony, S. M. Orsillo, & L. Roemer (Eds.), *Practitioner's guide to empirically-based measures of anxiety* (pp. 133–158). New York: Kluwer Academic/Plenum.

Antony, M. M., & Barlow, D. H. (2002). Specific phobia. In D. H. Barlow (Ed.), *Anxiety and its disorders: The nature and treatment of anxiety and panic* (2nd ed.) (pp. 380–417). New York: Guilford.

Antony, M. M., Brown, T. A., & Barlow, D. H. (1997a). Heterogeneity among specific phobia types in DSM-IV. *Behaviour Research and Therapy, 35,* 1089–1100.

Antony, M. M., Brown, T. A., & Barlow, D. H. (1997b). Response to hyperventilation and 5.5% CO_2 inhalation of subjects with types of specific phobia, panic disorder, or no mental disorder. *American Journal of Psychiatry, 154,* 1089–1095.

Antony, M. M., McCabe, R. E., Leeuw, I., Sano, N., & Swinson, R. P. (2001). Effect of exposure and coping style on in vivo exposure for specific phobia of spiders. *Behaviour Research and Therapy, 39,* 1137–1150.

Baker, B. L., Cohen, D. C., & Saunders, J. T. (1973). Self-directed desensitization for acrophobia. *Behaviour Research and Therapy, 11,* 79–89.

Bandura, A. (1977). Self-efficacy: Toward a unifying theory of behavioral change. *Psychological Review, 84,* 191–215.

Barlow, D. H. (1988). *Anxiety and its disorders: The nature and treatment of anxiety and panic.* New York: Guilford.

Barlow, D. H. (2002). *Anxiety and its disorders: The nature and treatment of anxiety and panic, second edition.* New York: Guilford.

Barlow, D.H. (2004). Psychological treatments. *American Psychologist, 59,* 869–878.

Barlow, D. H., & Craske, M.G. (2000). *Mastery of your anxiety and panic, third ed.* New York: Oxford University Press.

Barlow, D. H., Leitenberg, H., Agras, W. S., & Wincze, J. P. (1969). The transfer gap in systematic desensitization: An analogue study. *Behaviour Research and Therapy, 7,* 191–196.

Başoğlu, M., Marks, I. M., Kiliç, C., Brewin, C. R., & Swinson, R. P. (1994). Alprazolam and exposure for panic disorder with agoraphobia: Attribution of improvement to medication predicts subsequent relapse. *British Journal of Psychiatry, 164,* 652–659.

Beck, A. T. (1993). Cognitive therapy: Past, present, and future. *Journal of Consulting and Clinical Psychology, 61,* 194–198.

Beck, A. T., Emery, G., & Greenberg, R. L. (1985). *Anxiety disorders and phobias: A cognitive perspective.* New York: Basic Books.

Beckham, J.C., Vrana, S. R., May, J. G., Gustafson, D. J., & Smith, G. R. (1990). Emotional processing and fear measurement synchrony as indicators of treatment outcome in fear of flying. *Journal of Behavior Therapy and Experimental Psychiatry, 21,* 153–162.

Benjamin, J., Ben-Zion, I. Z., Karbofsky, E., & Dannon, P. (2000). Double-blind placebo-controlled pilot study of paroxetine for specific phobia. *Psychopharmacology, 149,* 194–196.

Booth, R., & Rachman, S. (1992). The reduction of claustrophobia-I. *Behaviour Research and Therapy, 30,* 207–221.

Bourque, P., & Ladouceur, R. (1980). An investigation of various performance-based treatments with acrophobics. *Behaviour Research and Therapy, 18,* 161–170.

Bouton, M. E. (1993). Context, time, and memory retrieval in the interference paradigms of Pavlovian learning. *Psychological Bulletin, 114,* 80–99.

Bouton, M. E., & Swartzentruber, D. (1991). Sources of relapse after extinction in Pavlovian and instrumental learning. *Clinical Psychology Review, 11,* 123–140.

Brown, D. (1996). *Flying without fear.* Oakland, CA: New Harbinger.

Brown, T. A., Di Nardo, P. A., Barlow, D. H. (1994). *Anxiety Disorders Interview Schedule for DSM–IV (ADIS–IV).* Albany, NY: Graywind.

Craske, M. G., Mohlman, J., Yi, J., Glover, D., & Valeri, S. (1995). Treatment of claustrophobias and snake/spider phobias: Fear of arousal and fear of context. *Behaviour Research and Therapy, 33,* 197–203.

Craske, M. G., & Mystkowski, J. L. (in press). Exposure therapy and extinction: Clinical studies. In M. G. Craske, D. Hermans, & D. Vansteenwegen (Eds.), *Fear and learning: From basic processes to clinical implications.* American Psychological Association.

Curtis, G. C., Magee, W. J., Eaton, W. W., Wittchen, H.-U., & Kessler, R. C. (1998). Specific fears and phobias: Epidemiology and classification. *British Journal of Psychiatry, 173,* 212–217.

Di Nardo, P. A., Guzy, L. T., & Bak, R. M. (1988). Anxiety response patterns and etiological factors in dog-fearful and non-fearful subjects. *Behaviour Research and Therapy, 26,* 245–251.

Eifert, G. H., & Forsyth, J. P. (2005). Acceptance and commitment therapy for anxiety disorders: A practitioner's treatment guide to using mindfulness, acceptance, and value-based behavior change strategies. Oakland, CA: New Harbinger.

Emmelkamp, P. M. G., & Felten, M. (1985). The process of exposure in vivo: Cognitive and physiological changes during treatment of acrophobia. *Behaviour Research and Therapy, 23,* 219–223.

Foa, E. B., Blau, J. S., Prout, M., & Latimer, P. (1977). Is horror a necessary component of flooding (implosion)? *Behaviour Research and Therapy, 15,* 397–402.

Foa, E. B. & Kozak, M. J. (1986). Emotional processing of fear: Exposure to corrective information. *Psychological Bulletin, 99,* 20–35.

Gauthier, J., & Marshall, W. L. (1977). The determination of optimal exposure to phobic stimuli in flooding therapy. *Behaviour Research and Therapy, 15,* 403–410.

Gitin, N. M., Herbert, J. D., & Schmidt, C. (1996, November). *One-session in vivo exposure for odontophobia.* Paper presented at the meeting of the Association for Advancement of Behavior Therapy, New York, NY.

Greenberg, D. B., Stern, T. A., & Weilburg, J. B. (1988). The fear of choking: Three successfully treated cases. *Psychosomatics, 29,* 126–129.

Hellström, K., Fellenius, J., & Öst, L.-G. (1996). One versus five sessions of applied tension in the treatment of blood phobia. *Behaviour Research and Therapy, 34,* 101–112.

Hellström, K., & Öst, L.-G. (1995). One-session therapist directed exposure vs. two forms of manual directed self-exposure in the treatment of spider phobia. *Behaviour Research and Therapy, 33,* 959–965.

Hermans, D., Craske, M. G., Mineka, S., & Lovibond, P. F. (in press). Extinction in human fear conditioning. *Biological Psychiatry.*

Himle, J. A., McPhee, K., Cameron, O. J., & Curtis, G. C. (1989). Simple phobia: Evidence for heterogeneity. *Psychiatry Research, 28,* 25–30.

Houlihan, D., Schwartz, C., Miltenberger, R., Heuton, D. (1993). The rapid treatment of a young man's balloon (noise) phobia using in vivo flooding. *Journal of Behavior Therapy and Experimental Psychiatry, 24,* 233–240.

Howard, W. A., Murphy, S. M., & Clarke, J. C. (1983). The nature and treatment of fear of flying: A controlled investigation. *Behavior Therapy, 14,* 557–567.

Institute of Medicine (2001). *Crossing the quality chasm: A new health system for the 21st century.* Washington, DC: National Academy.

Kendler, K. S., Neale, M. C., Kessler, R. C., Heath, A. C., & Eaves, L. J. (1992). The genetic epidemiology of phobias in women: The interrelationship of agoraphobia, social phobia, situational phobia, and simple phobia. *Archives of General Psychiatry, 39,* 273–281.

Kessler, R. C., Berglund, P., Demler, O., Jin, R., Merikangas, K. R., & Walters, E. E. (2005). Lifetime prevalence and age-of-onset distributions of DSM-IV disorders in the National Comorbidity Survey Replication. *Archives of General Psychiatry, 62,* 593–602.

Lang, A. J., & Craske, M. G. (2000). Manipulations of exposure-based therapy to reduce return of fear: A replication. *Behaviour Research and Therapy, 38,* 1–12.

Liddell, A., di Fazio, L., Blackwood, J., & Ackerman, C. (1994). Long-term follow-up of treated dental phobics. *Behaviour Research and Therapy, 32,* 605–610.

Marshall, W. L., Bristol, D., & Barbaree, H. E. (1992). Cognitions and courage in the avoidance behavior of acrophobics. *Behaviour Research and Therapy, 30,* 463–470.

Menzies, R. G., & Clarke, J. C. (1993). A comparison of in vivo and vicarious exposure in the treatment of childhood water phobia. *Behaviour Research and Therapy, 31,* 9–15.

Menzies, R. G., & Clarke, J. C. (1995). Danger expectancies and insight in acrophobia. *Behaviour Research and Therapy, 33,* 215–221.

Moore, R., and Brødsgaard, I. (1994). Group therapy compared with individual desensitization for dental anxiety. *Community Dentistry and Oral Epidemiology, 22,* 258–262.

Muris, P., Mayer, B., & Merckelbach, H. (1998). Trait anxiety as a predictor of behaviour therapy outcome in spider phobia. *Behavioural and Cognitive Psychotherapy, 26,* 87–91.

Mystkowski, J., Craske, M. G., & Echiverri, E. (2002) Treatment context and return of fear in spider phobia. *Behavior Therapy, 33,* 399–416.

Mystkowski, J., Echiverri, A., Labus, J., & Craske, M. G. (in press). Mental reinstatement of context and return of fear in spider phobia. *Behavior Therapy.*

Öst, L.-G. (1978). Behavioral treatment of thunder and lightning phobias. *Behaviour Research and Therapy, 16,* 197–207.

Öst, L.-G. (1987). Age of onset of different phobias. *Journal of Abnormal Psychology, 96,* 223–229.

Öst, L.-G. (1996). Long-term effects of behavior therapy for specific phobia. In M. R. Mavissakalian & R. F. Prien (Eds.), *Long-term treatments of anxiety disorders* (pp. 121–170). Washington, DC: American Psychiatric Press.

Öst, L.-G., Brandberg, M., & Alm, T. (1997). One versus five sessions of exposure in the treatment of flying phobia. *Behaviour Research and Therapy, 35,* 987–996.

Öst, L.-G., Fellenius, J., & Sterner, U. (1991). Applied tension, exposure in vivo, and tension-only in the treatment of blood phobia. *Behaviour Research and Therapy, 29,* 561–574.

Öst, L.-G., Ferebee, I., & Furmark, T. (1997). One-session group therapy of spider phobia: Direct versus indirect treatments. *Behaviour Research and Therapy, 35,* 721–732.

Öst, L.-G., Hellström, K., & Kaver, A. (1992). One versus five sessions of exposure in the treatment of injection phobia. *Behavior Therapy, 23,* 263–282.

Öst, L.-G., Johansson, J., & Jerremalm, A. (1982). Individual response patterns and the effects of different behavioral methods in the treatment of claustrophobia. *Behaviour Research and Therapy, 20,* 445–460.

Öst, L.-G., Salkovskis, P. M., & Hellström, K. (1991). One-session therapist directed exposure vs. self-exposure in the treatment of spider phobia. *Behavior Therapy, 22,* 407–422.

Öst, L.-G., & Sterner, U. (1987). Applied tension: A specific behavioral method for treatment of blood phobia. *Behaviour Research and Therapy, 25,* 25–29.

Page, A. C., and N. G. Martin. 1998. Testing a genetic structure of blood-injury-injection fears. *American Journal of Medical Genetics 81:*377–384.

Rachman, S. (1977). The conditioning theory of fear-acquisition: A critical examination. *Behaviour Research and Therapy, 15,* 375–387.

Ressler, K. J., Rothbaum, B. O., Tannenbaum, L., Anderson, P., Graap, K., Zimand, E., et al. (2004). Cognitive enhancers as adjuncts to psychotherapy: Use of D-cycloserine in phobic individuals to facilitate extinction of fear. *Archives of General Psychiatry, 61,* 1136–1144.

Rowe, M. K., & Craske, M. G. (1998). Effects of an expanding-spaced versus massed exposure schedule. *Behaviour Research and Therapy, 36,* 701–717.

Roy-Byrne, P., & Cowley, D. (in press). Pharmacological treatments for panic disorder, generalized anxiety disorder, specific phobia and social anxiety disorder. In P. E. Nathan and J. M. Gorman (Eds.), *A guide to treatments that work, third edition.* New York: Oxford University Press.

Ruhmland, M., & Margraf, J. (2001). Efficacy of psychological treatments for specific phobias and obsessive compulsive disorder. *Verhaltenstherapie, 11,* 14–26.

Seligman, M. E. P. (1971). Phobias and preparedness. *Behavior Therapy, 2,* 307–320.

Thorpe, S. J., & Salkovskis, P. M. (1995). Phobic beliefs: Do cognitive factors play a role in specific phobias? *Behaviour Research and Therapy, 33,* 805–816.

Tomarken, A. J., Mineka, S., & Cook, M. (1989). Fear-relevant selective associations and covariation bias. *Journal of Abnormal Psychology, 98,* 381–384.

Tsao, J. C. I., & Craske, M. G. (2001). Timing of treatment and return of fear: Effects of massed, uniform and expanding spaced exposure schedules. *Behavior Therapy, 31,* 479–497.

Vansteenwegen, D., Dirikx, T., Hermans, D., Vervliet, B., & Eelen, P. (2006). Renewal and reinstatement of fear: Evidence from human conditioning research. In M. G. Craske, D. Hermans, & D. Vansteenwegen (Eds.), *Fear and learning: From basic processes to clinical implications.* Washington, DC: American Psychological Association.

Walker, D. L., Ressler, K. J., Lu, K. T., & Davis, M. (2002). Facilitation of conditioned fear extinction by systemic administration or intra-amygdala infusions of D-cycloserine as assessed with fear-potentiated startle in rats. *Journal of Neuroscience, 22,* 2343–2351.

Wilhelm, F. H., & Roth, W. T. (1997). Acute and delayed effects of alprazolam on flight phobics during exposure. *Behaviour Research and Therapy, 35,* 831–841.

Williams, S. L. (1992). Perceived self-efficacy and phobic disability. In R. Schwarzer (Ed.), Self-efficacy: Thought control of action (pp. 149–176). Washington, DC: Hemisphere.

Williams, S. L., Dooseman, G., & Kleifield, E. (1984). Comparative effectiveness of guided mastery and exposure treatments for intractable phobias. *Journal of Consulting and Clinical Psychology, 52,* 505–518.

Williams, S. L., Kinney, P. J. & Falbo, J. (1989). Generalization of therapeutic changes in agoraphobia: The role of perceived self-efficacy. *Journal of Consulting and Clinical Psychology, 57,* 436–442.

Williams, S. L., Turner, S. M., & Peer, D. F. (1985). Guided mastery and performance desensitization treatments for severe acrophobia. *Journal of Consulting and Clinical Psychology, 53,* 237–247.

Williams, S. L., & Watson, N. (1985). Perceived danger and perceived self-efficacy as cognitive determinants of acrophobic behavior. *Behavior Therapy, 16,* 136–146.

Wittchen, H.-U. (1988). 1. Natural course and spontaneous remissions of untreated anxiety disorders: Results of the Munich Follow-up Study (MFS). In I. Hand & H.-U Wittchen (Eds.), *Panic and phobias 2: Treatment and variables affecting course and outcome* (pp. 3–17). New York: Springer-Verlag.

Wolpe, J. (1958). *Psychotherapy by reciprocal inhibition.* Stanford, CA: Stanford University Press.

About the Authors

Michelle G. Craske received her PhD from the University of British Columbia in 1985 and has authored more than 160 articles and chapters in the area of anxiety disorders. She has written books on the etiology and treatment of anxiety disorders, gender differences in anxiety, and translation from the basic science of fear learning to the clinical application of understanding and treating phobias, in addition to several self-help books. She has received continuous NIMH funding since 1991 for research projects pertaining to risk factors for anxiety disorders and depression among children and adolescents, the cognitive and physiological aspects of anxiety and panic attacks, and the development and dissemination of treatments for anxiety and related disorders. She is an associate editor for the *Journal of Abnormal Psychology* and *Behaviour Research and Therapy* and is a Scientific Board member for the Anxiety Disorders Association of America. She was a member of the *DSM–IV* Anxiety Disorders Work Group Subcommittee for revision of the diagnostic criteria surrounding panic disorder and specific phobia. Craske has given invited keynote addresses at many international conferences and is frequently invited to present training workshops on advances in the cognitive behavioral treatment of anxiety disorders. She is currently a professor in the Department of Psychology and Department of Psychiatry and Biobehavioral Sciences at UCLA and the director of the UCLA Anxiety Disorders Behavioral Research Program.

Martin M. Antony, PhD, is a professor in the Department of Psychology at Ryerson University in Toronto and is the director of research at the Anxiety Treatment and Research Centre at St. Joseph's Healthcare in Hamilton, Ontario. He received his doctorate in clinical psychology from the University at Albany, State University of New York, and completed his predoctoral internship training at the University of Mississippi Medical Center in Jackson, Mississippi. Antony has written 20 books and more than 100 articles and book chapters in the areas of cognitive behavioral therapy, obsessive-compulsive disorder, panic disorder, social phobia, and specific phobia. Antony has received career awards from the Society of Clinical Psychology (American Psychological Association), the Canadian Psychological Association, and the Anxiety Disorders Association of America, and is a fellow of the American and Canadian Psychological Associations. He has also served on the boards of directors for the Society of Clinical Psychology and the Association for Behavioral and Cognitive Therapies, and as program chair for past conventions of the Association for Advancement of Behavior Therapy and the Anxiety Disorders Association of America. Antony is actively involved in clinical research in the area of anxiety disorders and in teaching and education, and he maintains a clinical practice. He is also a diplomate in clinical psychology of the American Board of Professional Psychology.

David H. Barlow received his PhD from the University of Vermont in 1969 and has authored more than 500 articles and chapters, and close to 50 books and clinical workbooks, most in the area of emotional disorders and clinical research methodology. The books and workbooks have been translated into more than 20 languages, including Arabic, Mandarin, and Russian.

He was formerly a professor of psychiatry at the University of Mississippi Medical Center and a professor of psychiatry and psychology at Brown University and founded clinical psychology internships in both settings. He was also Distinguished Professor in the Department of Psychology at the University at Albany, State University of New York. Currently, he is a professor of psychology, a research professor of psychiatry, and the director of the Center for Anxiety and Related Disorders at Boston University.

Barlow received the 2000 American Psychological Association (APA) Distinguished Scientific Award for the Applications of Psychology. He also received the First Annual Science Dissemination Award from the Society for a Science of Clinical Psychology of the APA and the 2000 Distinguished Scientific Contribution Award from the Society of Clinical Psychology of the APA. He also received an award in appreciation of outstanding achievements from the General Hospital of the Chinese

People's Liberation Army, Beijing, China, with an appointment as Honorary Visiting Professor of Clinical Psychology. During the 1997/1998 academic year, he was the Fritz Redlich Fellow at the Center for Advanced Study in Behavioral Sciences in Palo Alto, California.

Other awards include career contribution awards from the Massachusetts, California, and Connecticut Psychological Associations; the 2004 C. Charles Burlingame Award from the Institute of Living in Hartford, Connecticut; the First Graduate Alumni Scholar Award from the Graduate College at the University of Vermont; the Masters and Johnson Award from the Society for Sex Therapy and Research; G. Stanley Hall Lectureship, American Psychological Association; a certificate of appreciation for contributions to women in clinical psychology from Section IV of Division 12 of the APA, the Clinical Psychology of Women; and a MERIT award from the National Institute of Mental Health for long-term contributions to the clinical research effort. He is a past president of the Society of Clinical Psychology of the American Psychological Association and the Association for the Advancement of Behavior Therapy, a past editor of the journals *Behavior Therapy, Journal of Applied Behavior Analysis,* and *Clinical Psychology: Science and Practice,* and is currently editor-in-chief of the Treatments *ThatWork*™ series for Oxford University Press.

He was chair of the American Psychological Association Task Force of Psychological Intervention Guidelines, a member of the *DSM–IV* Task Force of the American Psychiatric Association, and a co-chair of the working group for revising the anxiety disorder categories. He is also a diplomate in clinical psychology of the American Board of Professional Psychology and maintains a private practice.